Scotland's
Forgotten Past

Alistair Moffat

Scotland's Forgotten Past

A History of the Mislaid, Misplaced and Misunderstood

with 37 illustrations

Contents

Introduction

Until very recently, much of Scotland's long history seems to have been forgotten, misplaced or misunderstood, and often thought of as incidental. In the past, the past was much simpler. During drowsy double periods on a Friday afternoon, Scottish schoolchildren watched a procession of kings, queens, warriors and saints shuffle across the landscape before eventually and inevitably arriving at now. Far in the distance we heard the clash and war cries of ancient battles and saw fire and destruction flicker on the horizon, but we were not diverted as nations formed and comfortable destinies were settled.

Scotland's history was simpler than most. There wasn't much of it, and in any case the most interesting bits happened when it collided with England's. The cheering after the Battle of Bannockburn in 1314 somehow died away and led to the disaster at Flodden in 1513. From there we made it safely to the Union of the Crowns in 1603, and then to the Union of the Parliaments in 1707. Bonnie Prince Charlie briefly objected in 1745/6, but thereafter everything calmed down, thank goodness, and Scotland's history became part of Britain's history. There were walk-on parts for Scottish inventors from James Watt to John Logie Baird, scientists like Alexander Fleming and James Clerk Maxwell, writers like Walter Scott and Robert Louis Stevenson and the occasional plucky victory at Twickenham or Wembley. But that was basically that. Until recently.

Generations of Scots cheerfully failed to notice how profoundly our history had been hijacked by our friends in the south. Queen Margaret, the only famous Scotswoman before Mary, Queen of Scots (who was essentially French as well as feckless), was English. Married to Malcolm Canmore, a bearded, carousing Celtic warrior-king, she brought civilization and better table manners to his hall at Dunfermline, substituting prayer and piety for roaring, drunken feasting, and was of course made a saint. Her son, David I, was raised as a Norman Frenchman in England, and behind him trailed processions of French monks who built the Border Abbeys and brought more civilization to the blasted heaths of the north. Even our heroes appeared to be on loan. William Wallace was known as Le Waleis, 'the Welshman', and lots of Robert de Brus' Norman French relatives fought against him at Bannockburn. Far from a nation-defining victory, it could also be seen as more of a family tiff.

Even when it was occasionally written down, our history was not our own. It used routinely to begin with the arrival of the Romans in the 1st century AD, because Tacitus' *Agricola* was the sole surviving written source for the doings of the rain-soaked, woad-covered natives. But even then, they were ignored. Most Scots were too busy admiring the might of Rome, the shining armour, the red cloaks and tremendous plumed helmets of the legions – images fed by the sword-and-sandal epics turned out by Hollywood – to notice that Tacitus was also writing about our ancestors and our landscape, and not always in glowing terms. The truth is many of us would rather have been the descendants of the Romans than the scruffy Caledonians. They got regularly stuffed anyway, a rabble of ululating savages scattered by the iron discipline of Agricola's soldiers at Mons Graupius, wherever that was.

In fact, until the late 20th century, histories of Scotland often began not with the people who lived there but with invaders who came from somewhere else, ignoring eight millennia of our prehistory and opening with the defeat of our ancestors by an army that had marched from the south. A theme seemed to develop as the Venerable Bede wrote of the expansion of Northumbria into southern Scotland. Macbeth became famous only because William Shakespeare wrote about him. And he came to a sticky end. Having raised an army in England and with the help of Siward, Earl of Northumbria, Malcolm arrives to clear up the blood-spattered mess and restore Scotland to civilization.

As we dutifully copied down in our jotters the dates of disasters (and the one home win) from Flodden to Culloden, the impression was not just that we were in bed with an elephant, but that it rolled over often, too often. Surely it was better to hitch our history to the English juggernaut, especially when the drive for empire began in earnest in the second half of the 18th century. Rather than charging across the heather, claymores raised, to attack yet another government army sent from the south, surely it was more sensible to be rewarded by that government for charging the native armies on the battlefields of India, South Africa and beyond. Exotic battle honours were soon stitched onto the standards of Scottish regiments, and fortunes made in the Raj and the forests of Canada that raised great mansions on wide estates from the Borders to the Highlands. But it didn't last. When the winds of change began to blow harder in the 1950s and the sun set very quickly on the British Empire, our gaze was at last turned inwards.

About thirty years ago, Scottish history writing suddenly began to flower, perhaps in part because of the simultaneous rise of a nationalism that dragged a national awareness behind it. And it turned out that actually, we were different, we did have a much more complex and much richer story hidden under all the tartan blankets for sale on Edinburgh's Royal Mile.

I began writing about Scotland's story in 1999, and twenty-five books later I find that my curiosity is nowhere near exhausted. I remain fascinated, still writing about this quirky, bad-tempered little nation on the northwest edge of Europe, still discovering new insights, untold stories, and things I don't understand.

That's so for a simple reason. The story is still in the process of becoming known, and much waits to be revealed about our ancestors and the land they made.

For this book, I've chosen thirty-six episodes, half-forgotten or misunderstood tales that had been submerged by the wash of history across the country. They are arranged in chronological order, link to each other and, I hope, avoid falling into the bear-traps of cliché. They show how different Scotland is and was, but their guiding principle for me was always *Really? I didn't know that.*

1 The Primeval Pile-Up

 On a sunny summer's evening in 1989, Patricia Macdonald took a photograph that explains Scotland's history. From an aeroplane flying over Loch Lomond, she noticed how the long shadows played on Conic Hill's northeastern shore. They threw into relief a corrugated, buckled ridge that climbed up out of the water before stretching away into the distance across high moorland. To the south of the ridge the land was green, a patchwork of fields, farmhouses and woods, and to the north it glowed with the russet colours of the heather-clad uplands where the mountains began to rise.

What Dr Macdonald captured so brilliantly was a snapshot of Scotland's geological makeup. The buckled ridge is a cultural, political and agricultural frontier. It is the line of the Highland Boundary Fault that runs between two Scotlands, from Kintyre in the southwest to Stonehaven on the North Sea coast. To the south of the fault lies the rich farmland of the Midland Valley, where most of the population has always lived, and to the north are the mountains, the glens and the straths, with a very different history, a different language and a different people.

Hundreds of millions of years ago, when the planet was young, its crust was in constant movement. As volcanoes roared and tsunamis thundered across the oceans, vast palaeocontinents with exotic, science fiction-like names were moving slowly across the face of the Earth. Avalonia, Laurentia and Baltica were pushed by tectonic forces as they formed, submerged, rose up, splintered and reformed. Sometimes bits broke off. These slivers of ancient rock are known as terranes, and the landmass of Scotland is an amalgam of four, a nation of fragments, geological leavings. A series of more or less parallel faultlines show the northeast to southwest angle of the collision of these bits and pieces.

The northwesternmost and the oldest terrane formed the Western Isles, Coll, Tiree and Iona as well as much of the northern Atlantic coastline. Its basis is an ancient rock called Lewissian gneiss. Very hard and formed deep in the fiery bowels of the Earth, it can be seen in outcrops as far north as Cape Wrath and on the western peninsula of Islay known as the Rhinns in the south.

East of the coastal faultline lie the remains of a second terrane, whose southeastern edge runs along the very obvious boundary that is the Great Glen. It stretches from Inverness down to Fort William and beyond. Below it is a third splinter of primeval rock, and its edges were those photographed by Patricia Macdonald over Loch Lomond. The fertile Midland Valley came drifting across the crust of the Earth from tropical latitudes. Over cycles of millions of years of dense jungle, countless trees fell and were compressed into seams of coal. Aeons later, these would form the basis of Scotland's Industrial Revolution in the 18th and 19th centuries.

At the hamlet of Niarbyl on the west coast of the Isle of Man, a thin, grey-white seam of rock rises out of the waters of the Irish Sea. It is the only place where the precise moment of Britain's most spectacular geological collision can be clearly seen. Known as the Iapetus Suture, it is a memory of a vanished ocean. Lying between the ancient continents of Laurentia and Avalonia, the

Iapetus Ocean began to shrink as these vast landmasses drew closer and closer about 410 million years ago. The four terranes that would become Scotland had formed part of the southeastern shore of Laurentia, and they were slowly bulldozed into the northeastern edge of Avalonia. Attached to it were the rock formations that would become England, Wales and Southern Ireland.

In keeping with the clichés of recorded history, to say nothing of modern attitudes, Scotland's terranes were harder than those of the soft south and when the palaeocontinents collided, the northern rocks forced the southern to buckle like a disintegrating rugby scrum, upending the strata and pushing valuable seams of coal and iron ore much closer to the surface. This showed that Scotland being harder than England was not necessarily to the detriment of the latter. Scotland's part of the seismic bargain was the windswept moorland of the Southern Uplands, while England's industry would flourish on top of the Northumbrian, Durham and Cumbrian coalfields.

Fire and ice began to move mountains. As the Earth shuddered and volcanoes sent vast amounts of ejecta rocketing into the sky, the Atlantic Ocean was forming. It eventually submerged a ring of volcanoes that ran from St Kilda to Ailsa Craig. The wide caldera of others can be clearly seen on the Ardnamurchan peninsula on the mainland and on Skye.

Much later, about 2.4 million years ago, the ice came. Probably caused by slight variations in the shape of the Earth's orbit around the sun, several ice ages locked up the land in their frigid grip. The most recent has only just ended. Some 15,000 thousand years ago, ice sheets more than a kilometre thick crushed Scotland and the north of England. As incessant winds blew over the brilliant white landscape, our geography lay dormant, waiting to be formed, waiting to make our history.

When the Earth's orbit around the sun at last moved back into kilter about 11,000 years ago, the weather grew warmer and very rapidly the ice began to melt and to move. The spine of Scotland, the Drumalban mountains, stretching north from Ben Lomond to Assynt, lay under a vast, hemispherical ice dome. When it began to splinter, the great weight of the ice moved like a gigantic white harrow over the landscape, bulldozing it into the shape we recognize on today's maps. Glaciers ground their way both west and eastwards down the slopes of the Drumalban mountains. On their undersides, they carried along a great deal of rocky debris and they scraped and shaped the land. Glaciers moving east were stopped and split by the very hard volcanic rock on which Stirling Castle now sits. When it divided, the glacier left a crag tail on the eastern, leeward side of the rock, where the town of Stirling grew up in the shelter of its great castle. Something very similar happened when the ice river reached Edinburgh's Castle Rock.

As the heavy blanket of the ice dome was at last lifted, the land began to rise. In what is known as isostatic uplift, the crust of the Earth bounced back. With the great melt, sea levels also rose, sometimes faster than the land. Around 5,000 BC the Firth of Clyde broke through into Loch Lomond and almost made a link with the Firth of Forth. Only a narrow land bridge east of Aberfoyle prevented northern Scotland from becoming an island. Instead of a channel of seawater, a wide swathe of treacherous marshland was formed. Known as Flanders Moss, it presented a real barrier, a boggy frontier between north and south. In his biography of Agricola, Tacitus wrote that when the Romans advanced into Caledonia, the legions were marching 'as if into another island'. Geology and the ice made that narrow neck of land a strategic hinge that was guarded for centuries by Stirling Castle, brooding in its glacier-carved rock.

To the east, isostatic uplift had a spectacular effect. 8,000 years ago, there was no North Sea. When the ice domes over Scandinavia melted, the Earth's crust to the south bounced back and between Denmark, Germany, the Low Countries and the east coast of Britain there was dry land, a wide subcontinent archaeologists call Doggerland. What is now the Dogger Bank, a large sandbank off the east coast of England, was once a range of northern hills. The valleys, rivers and lakes of Doggerland sustained substantial communities of hunter-gatherers, and after the ice, some of the first pioneers who came to Scotland walked across what is now the bed of the North Sea.

Far to the northwest, a volcano roared and a huge eruption sent millions of cubic tonnes of ejecta into the atmosphere, so much that a dust cloud obscured the sun. On Iceland, Mount Hekla blew itself apart in 1159 BC, the precise date traceable by the measurement of ancient tree rings. As skies darkened, a volcanic winter lasting eighteen years followed, and it had a catastrophic effect on the communities of the Hebrides and the Atlantic seaboard. As the land withered into a wet, sunless, toxic wasteland, many fled over the mountain passes to the east. As peat began to form and cultivable land shrivelled, more refugees were driven from their island and coastal homes.

Climate and geology have had a determinant effect on Scotland's history. The uniquely diverse set of habitats created by the four terranes has meant that our culture and history has itself been diverse. Beween east and west, north and south, upland and lowland, coastal and inland, many Scotlands have developed distinct identities that resist tartan pigeon-holing and easy assumptions. The Scots are indeed different from the English but often they are even more different from each other. Geology, fire and ice formed the mosaic that makes up the story of Scotland.

2 The Great Halls

 After the white wasteland of the ice had shrunk back to the far north, Scotland quickly grew green. As with the Arctic tundra now, summer brought warmth and the land was carpeted with sweet grass. Herds of wild horses, deer and other fauna followed the seasonal grazing, and behind them came the hunters, the pioneers, the first to see the mountains, glens, rivers and straths of Scotland. Then the trees began to grow. Only a short time after the retreat of the glaciers, a dense wildwood covered the land and under its canopy people began to settle, making summer camps, gathering the wild harvest of autumn and wrapping their furs against the cold blast of winter.

It is likely that there were very few pioneers living in what is now Scotland in the millennia after the ice. Populations increased only very slowly, and hunter-gatherer bands needed wide ranges to sustain themselves. In some ways it was a good life, when the roots, fruits, nuts and berries were plentiful and game was abundant. On sunny evenings, with full bellies, and a good summer to come, our ancestors will have sat together, paddling their feet in the burn, telling stories and teasing each other.

But around 4,000 BC, life in the wildwood was changed utterly. Immigrants crossed the North Sea, and in their boats they carried the seeds of the greatest revolution in human history. The first farmers made landfall on the eastern shores of Scotland, moved up the great rivers, claimed good land and built structures that astonished the native hunter-gatherers.

1976 saw the one of the driest, sunniest and warmest summers on record. From the middle of June to the end of August, temperatures regularly rose to more than 30°C and the tarmac on roads melted. Snowploughs were sent out from Inverness on the A9 to spray the surface with sand. There was widespread drought, and yet, at the Royal Commission for Ancient and Historic Monuments in Scotland, there was great delight. By coincidence, the RCAHMS began an annual programme of aerial photography in the same year, and droughts show up crop marks very well. Wheat and oats are particularly

sensitive to soil water content and in dry summers features such as ditches or post-holes that may be invisible on the ground can be seen clearly from the air.

During the hot summer of 1976, an aerial survey was systematically covering the lower valley of the River Dee near Aberdeen. Over a field of corn at Balbridie on the south bank of the river, a photograph was taken that showed something remarkable. It was a series of rows of post-holes in the shape of a large rectangular building that measured 25 by 13 metres (82 by 43 feet). Then, a short time later, the remains of a second building were found. Only about a mile away, on the north bank of the Dee at Crathes, there was another set of post-holes from another huge building.

At first, the archaeologists at Balbridie were certain that they were excavating a hall from the Dark Ages, the sort of

feasting hall so vividly described in *Beowulf.* At Yeavering, some 200 miles (320 kilometres) to the south, in Northumberland, an Anglo-Saxon hall of a similar size had been discovered. But when the remains of charred grains were radiocarbon-dated, the excavators were astonished to discover that the structure at Balbridie had been built almost 4,500 years earlier.

Nothing like it had been seen before. For the hunter-gatherers who fished the River Dee and hunted along its wooded banks, this huge building with a roof that rose up to 10 metres (33 feet) would have been almost incomprehensible, the work of giants or the gods. It was as though the natives had emerged from their shelters among the shadows of the trees to see a skyscraper.

Not technologically very different from the Anglo-Saxon halls of the Dark Ages, the buildings at Balbridie and Crathes may have had no contemporary parallel in Scotland, but the remains of others have been found across the Northern European Plain, in Poland, Germany and Holland. In their boats, the first farmers carried not only seed but also expertise. They knew how to erect high walls and make them stable in post-holes, form roof trusses and secure them with ridge poles, and they had the tools to do these things. At Crathes, the long walls were made from oak trees, either entire trunks or split timbers. These could only have been felled by the very best and biggest flint axes and worked with chisels of extremely hard and sharp stone tapped by wooden mallets. All of these skills crossed the North Sea with the early farmers, and they transformed the landscape.

Each of the halls on the Dee was home to between thirty and fifty people, substantial communities far larger than hunter-gatherer bands. But they needed to be fed from the moment they hauled up their boats onto the riverbank. Until they had cleared the land, most probably by burning back the scrub and planting in the rich potash left behind, they too needed to hunt and gather the wild harvest. That will have meant competition with native bands, perhaps even conflict. But once the great trees were felled, the halls built, crops sown in the small fields around them and pens made for such stock as they had, something more than a farm was established. Ownership of land began to replace the customary rights that the native hunter-gatherers had over their wide ranges.

There is likely to have been resistance of some kind, but analyses of ancestral DNA show that the incomers quickly overwhelmed the natives by sheer numbers, and they did so for an unexpected reason. Having quickly become true Scots, they invented porridge.

Populations of hunter-gatherer bands grew only very slowly. These people were highly mobile, barely rustling the leaves of the wildwood as they moved through it, leaving only gossamer traces of their passing. As they hunted in the woods or waited quietly in clearings, their spears and bows at the ready, they needed to travel light. From summer to winter camps, following the seasons around large areas, they could not carry or cope easily with little children. But in any case, natural biological cycles precluded large families.

The diet of these bands was difficult for babies and toddlers to chew and digest. Their infant teeth were too soft for the roots and fruits, and meat that may often have been tough. For that reason, hunter-gatherer mothers breastfed their children for much longer than was customary in farming communities, perhaps until the age of three or four. Mothers' milk was the sole source of the Class I protein that growing children need. Nursing a baby or a toddler usually means that women cannot conceive, and in that way, nature kept a balance. Our ancestors lived much shorter lives and few reached the age of thirty. For a woman, that meant a fertile period of only fourteen to sixteen years at the most, and of course not all of her babies would have survived, and nor might she. One hypothesis holds that the prime cause of death in prehistoric women was complications in childbirth. And so for all these reasons, the population of Palaeolithic Scotland was tiny.

Porridge changed that. The cereals grown in the little fields around the halls on the banks of the Dee were used to make unleavened bread, and also ground into a nutritious paste that was mixed with water or milk. This form of porridge could be spooned into the mouths of infants from an early age, and it meant that they could be weaned more quickly. This made the birth interval much shorter, and whereas a native hunter-gatherer mother might hope to have four children at most, with perhaps two or three surviving, the women who lived in the warmth and shelter of the great halls could have twice as many. In this way, the first farmer population expanded rapidly and quickly overwhelmed the natives, driving them deeper into the interior to survive as best they could in less hospitable country.

But there arose a substantial difficulty, and that was disease. Because farmers lived in close and constant proximity to animals (although there was no evidence that parts of the halls were used as byres for overwintering), their diseases jumped the species barrier. Tuberculosis, measles and smallpox originated in cattle, and if the farmers drank cows' milk, it was a fatally simple matter to ingest the pathogens. Pigs transmitted influenza and whooping cough. The immigrants did eventually develop resistance to these diseases, but it may be that at Balbridie and Crathes, these early settlers suffered badly.

One of the many surprising discoveries on these fascinating sites is that despite the immense investment of labour in building them, the halls stood for only a short time. For only ninety or so years, perhaps less, families lived under the big roofs – until they decided to burn them down.

There are hints that the halls were more than housing. Before the main structure was raised at Crathes, it seems that the farmers set up two totem poles. Along the axis of what would become the hall, they dug two post-holes and set up two tall timbers that would not be needed to hold up the roof. Perhaps they were the focus of worship of some kind, of reverence for the great trees that had been cut down to create the building.

When the leaders of the communities reached a decision, perhaps prompted by too many outbreaks of illness, they set fire to the halls. They will have blazed bright, been seen for miles, maybe even by the gods. At Balbridie, a great deal of corn, much more than would have been accidentally dropped, was incinerated. This may have been an offering. It was the corn that helped establish the first farmers, made their porridge, ensured that they thrived and drove out the natives. Perhaps they gave some of this bounty back to their gods.

3 The Cave of the Headless Children

At high tide the cliff and its caves could not be reached except by boat. Even at the summer solstice, when the sun in the north did not set but danced along the night horizon, its rays never shone into the deep darkness. But the gods were there, and when the people came, they brought the children to the cave. In the silence and the stillness there was ceremony, chanting, and above all reverence for the gods, for they were close. In flickering, torch-lit shadows, priests raised their axes high and decapitated the little ones who had been brought to them. Their severed heads were spitted on sharp stakes and set upright in the sand and the shale at the mouth of the cave. Their sightless eyes gazed across a grey sea to an eternal horizon.

These things happened. In Scotland. As part of some unknowable religious rite, our ancestors had their children's heads cut off.

In 1929, Sylvia Benton and a team of local excavators came to what is known as the Sculptor's Cave. Its two entrances lie at the foot of a sea cliff on the southern shore of the Moray Firth at Covesea, between Lossiemouth and Burghead. Benton recorded finds of 1,800 disarticulated human bones in the cave and concluded that, like the great tombs on Orkney, it had been used as an ossuary. The cervical vertebrae, the neck bones, of children were found to have clear cut-marks on them. For reasons that could only be guessed at, these young people had been decapitated in or at the mouth of the cave where all could see. It is probable that they were dead before losing their heads. Perhaps their bodies had been brought to the sea cliff by grieving parents to complete some sort of funerary rite. It may have been that these were the children of important people whose deaths merited special ceremony because they were thought to have power after life, but that is no more than an extension of an already shaky hypothesis.

In 1979, a second archaeological dig began at the Sculptor's Cave. More careful, painstaking and rigorous, this investigation found something remarkable. At the mouth of the cave, Ian and Alexandra Shepherd, the team leaders, came across the small lower jawbones of several children. They were contemporary with the cervical vertebrae found by Sylvia Benton. It seems that once the heads had been spitted on stakes and set up outside, the elements did their work. As hair and flesh fell away in the frost and the winter winds and the skulls were exposed, it appears that the lower jawbones dropped to the ground, perhaps in periods of especially severe weather. What surprised and disappointed the Shepherds was the fact that despite a thorough search, no skulls were found. But strangely, there was some slight evidence that the severed heads may have been decorated in some way.

The walls of the cave gave it its name. There are several relief carvings of characteristic Pictish symbols: a V-rod, a crescent, a fish-like creature and other abstract designs of the sort often found on upright stones not only in Moray but all over north-eastern Scotland. The carvings in the cave were done some time between the 2nd and 4th centuries AD.

Evidence was found of more decapitations carried out approximately twelve centuries after the earlier rituals took place. Only one child lost their head and all the others were adults. This second phase of beheadings seems to have had a different significance, and archaeologists have interpreted them as executions. However all that may be, it is both strange and striking that such a continuity, however extended, should be maintained. Over all that long time, was there a memory of the cave as a setting for ritual decapitation, either spiritual or judicial?

The sea cliff is an otherworldly place, strange and desolate. The rock is heavily eroded, ridged, wind- and wave-worn. And the vistas to the north, across the Moray Firth, are bleak. Like all such places, the Sculptor's Cave is damp, dark and uncomfortable. There are two entrances to parallel passages, and some distance into the left-hand one (the other was boarded up) there is a large, smooth stone with some 21st-century offerings laid on it. Bird skulls, rabbit bones, pebbles and other bits and pieces have been carefully placed there by visitors. For whatever reason, this dark place still retains its ancient power, a pungent genius loci.

It is impossible to recreate the rituals that took place. But equally, it is too easy to be appalled at the image of a priest hacking off the head of a child. It seems to us an act of barbarism, but it might also have been seen as an act of devotion.

Celtic societies in Western Europe may have believed that the essence of a person, what others might call the soul, lay not in the heart but in the head. At Lochend, near Edinburgh, a multiple burial dating to the 1st or 2nd centuries AD was found. The remains of at least twenty adults and one child were recognized, but seven skulls were missing. An examination of the cervical vertebrae revealed that these headless people had been decapitated. In loose earth near the burial, six skulls were recovered.

Had they been set up there for display, perhaps spitted on stakes long ago decayed?

After AD 70, the Romans moved north to bring the territory of the Brigantes, a confederation of kindreds who straddled the Pennines, into the empire. At Stanwick, near Scotch Corner, the legions attacked a native fort and overwhelmed it. Among the debris in the ditch below the ramparts, archaeologists found skulls, but no skeletons associated with them. In any case, the skulls seemed much older than the date of the battle at Stanwick Fort. It seems that the Brigantes' priests, who we might call druids, had set up a row of skulls on the rampart. Perhaps these had been important and powerful people, and perhaps they could help repel the Romans. It was what one writer has called a ghost fence.

Archaeologists have discovered a second significant cave in the sea cliff, not far from the Sculptor's Cave. It seems that its dark interior was lit by similar rituals and many bones have been found. Were these places on the Moray Firth coast portals to other worlds? Only accessible at low tide, they were certainly liminal, perhaps understood as being on an edge between the temporal world and the spiritual, between the land of the living and the land of the dead. When the ceremonies had ended and the people had gone, leaving behind the bodies and the bones of their dead, and the tide had rushed in, did the gods come to the caves?

Very little is known for certain about the beliefs of our ancestors, but some aspects may be safely assumed. Just as Christians do, they believed in an afterlife of some kind, and that in turn persuaded them that death was not an end but a transition. And how the living managed that transition on behalf of their dead was important.

It is also likely that like many religions, theirs understood different spheres. The visible, temporal world of the living lay between the gods of the earth and water and the gods in the skies. What can be added to these generalizations is something less obvious. Western culture has become used to the notion of a New Testament God of love and forgiveness, but many other pantheons were not like that. Gods could be malicious, and even vengeful. They often demanded sacrifice and propitiation. The gods of Greece and Rome squabbled with each other and meddled directly in the affairs of the living, sometimes wreaking havoc. In the Old Testament, God commanded a blood sacrifice, demanding that Abraham cut his son's throat on an altar before relenting at the last minute. Some medieval illustrations show Abraham wielding a sword, about to decapitate Isaac.

The caves at the foot of the sea cliff on the Moray coast may have been seen as a twilight zone, a place between worlds where the living brought their dead and where, in a series of unknowable rituals, they communed with their gods. Perhaps they also made sacrifice, invoking divine protection against evil, against malign gods who might send storms to destroy crops or disease to decimate communities. If the caves were the shadowy place of the old gods, where the bones of the dead were kept safe, then perhaps they needed to be defended. When the priests cut off the heads of the little children, the innocents, and spitted them on stakes at the mouth of the holy cave, were they building a ghost fence?

Many of us may be the direct descendants of these early peoples of Scotland, and it is probable that, allowing for the effects of modern medicine, dentistry and sanitation, we look like them. But our ancestors were different from us, very different. That simple recognition should persuade us not to judge them by our standards and shudder at the treatment of the children in the Sculptor's Cave, but to try to understand them better.

4 High Noon on Lewis

 On a sunny day on the Isle of Lewis, not far from the standing stones at Calanais, a Greek explorer fitted together a gnomon. Taking three lengths of wood, he made from them a right-angled triangle and set it on its edge on flat ground so that it was steady. As every schoolboy and girl (and Pythagoras) knows, the right angle ensured that one of the short sides would be perfectly perpendicular to the base. When the sun was at its zenith at midday, the Greek took a measurement of latitude so that he could tell how far north he had travelled.

Pytheas had begun his great journey into the unknown from his home city of Massalia, modern Marseille, some time around 320 BC. It was a thriving merchant town, established in about 600 BC as a colony by Greeks who had migrated from the western coasts of Turkey. Before he set out, probably taking a land route across France to the Atlantic shore, Pytheas had used his gnomon to take a baseline reading of latitude, and as he moved further and further north, he made sure to take regular measurements. One of the most northerly readings he recorded places him on the Isle of Lewis, off the Atlantic coast of Scotland. Pytheas was one of the first southerners, among many who would come over the centuries that followed, to record what he found north of the Cheviots.

Tin was what initially attracted the attention of the mercantile community of Massalia. It was an essential ingredient in the valuable alloy of bronze, and it was rare. Herodotus, the Greek geographer and historian, knew of a place he called the *Kassiterides*, the 'Tin Islands', but that was all. 'I cannot speak with any certainty,' he wrote, 'but they may lie somewhere in the Northern Sea.' Tin was very valuable, and it may be that Pytheas set out for the northern islands to find out more and make contacts. Commerce as much as curiosity may have persuaded him to travel a very long way from home to places that outran all contemporary knowledge.

Place-names often tell stories. Most likely when Pytheas reached the southern shores of the English Channel, he asked the native people the name of the big island that lay across the narrow sea. 'Pretannike,' they replied, 'It is called Pretannike.' That is how the Greek traveller rendered the first-ever historical reference to the name of Britain. Our version derives from Britannia, the name of the Roman province, which itself comes from Pretannike.

It means something. The people who told Pytheas the name of the big island spoke Gaulish, a Celtic language, and in it *pretani* means 'the painted people'. Gaulish is long extinct, but it was close to early forms of Welsh in the 4th century BC, and the name survives in the modern language as *Ynys Prydein*, the Island of Britain. The reference is likely to speak of something more permanent than warpaint, and is probably best translated as 'the tattooed people'.

When Pytheas returned to Massalia, he gathered together all of his readings, notes and impressions into what was called a *periplus*. This means a 'sail-round', a voyage and a guide for mariners. That was one of the reasons he had set up his gnomon on the Isle of Lewis and at many other locations. Recordings of latitude in unknown territories would greatly assist those who followed in Pytheas' wake.

As he circumnavigated Britain, rounding its three corners, the explorer kept a record of how far his ship (or ships or boats on which he had bought a passage) travelled in a day before its skipper found safe haven as darkness fell. Early mariners did not sail at night. Such calculations must have been very difficult, especially when Pytheas' voyage threaded its way through the sounds, narrows and sea lochs of the Hebrides and the Atlantic shore. The changing strengths of the winds and tides will have influenced progress greatly. Perhaps he consulted the skipper or the steersman of whichever craft he sailed in. Pytheas measured his progress in Greek *stades*, a distance of about 185 metres (600 feet). It was the circumference of the ancient stadium at Olympia, and also the derivation of the modern word. When Pytheas returned to Massalia, he added up all of the distances he believed he had travelled and found that Britain was 40,000 *stades* in circumference. In modern measurement, that came to 4,600 miles (7,400 kilometres). His calculation was astonishingly accurate. The length of the British coastline is 4,710 miles (7,580 kilometres). Such precision lends a great deal of credibility to Pytheas' account of early Scotland.

His book was known as *On the Ocean*, and it became very widely read. The ocean was thought to be a dangerous place. To those used to the enclosed geography of the Mediterranean, where ships rarely had to sail out of the comforting sight of land, the vastness of the mighty Atlantic was terrifying. What lay beyond it? What creatures lurked in its dark depths? But Pytheas was not dismayed; his curiosity, and perhaps his commercial acumen, overcame his terror. Not for nothing was

his statue placed on the façade of the stock exchange in Marseille in the 19th century.

Unlike Tacitus' *Agricola,* the text of *On the Ocean* has not survived. Its contents are known only through its frequent quotation in the writings of other ancient authors. Pytheas' observations about Britain are fascinating, a first recorded glimpse of what he saw as he circumnavigated the three corners of Kent, Cornwall and Orkney. The island was 'too much subject to the Bear', he wrote, meaning that Britain, and especially the north, was very cold. Ursula Major, the Great She-Bear, was a constellation well known to the Greeks and the Romans, and they knew that its stars lit the northern skies.

Pytheas probably travelled with local guides as he made his way around the coasts, but he may not have needed them to act as translators unless dialects were particularly impenetrable. Around the colony of Massalia, the native kindreds spoke Gaulish, and some of the earliest personal names known in this language, which lacked a script of its own, were rendered in Greek letters. Gaulish and early Welsh, which was spoken all over mainland Britain (but not Ireland), were almost certainly mutually intelligible. Perhaps this was helpful to Pytheas, since despite being a stranger and no doubt looking different, he never mentions being in any danger. 'The natives are ruled by many kings or princes who are at peace with each other,' he noted, 'and they live in thatched houses and store their grain underground.' They also ate plain fare and were 'of simple manners', observed the sophisticate from the civilized south, 'and they fight from chariots.'

These remarks are the first in a long line. Pytheas was patronizing, clearly considering himself a superior sort, but compared to Tacitus 400 years later, he was at least curious about the people he met. The Roman senator, of course, saw the kindreds of the north, the Caledonians and others, as enemies, as barbarians, and thought them very primitive. He confirmed Pytheas' observation that many small kingdoms existed and that the high-born fought in chariots. And he hated the weather. 'The climate is miserable, with frequent rain and mists,' Tacitus complained, wrapping his cloak around his shoulders. But when it came to the influence of the Ocean on northern Scotland, he was both accurate and eloquent: 'Nowhere is the dominance of the sea more extensive. There are many tidal currents, flowing in different directions. They do not merely rise as far as the shoreline and recede again. They flow far inland, wind around, and push themselves among the highlands and mountains, as if in their own realm.'

Pytheas' recording of the name of Pretannike and its later rendering as Britannia was never forgotten, and it gave rise to an enduring image that remembered its origins. In the late 17th century, the figure of Britannia was created so that it could be stamped on coins and used elsewhere. Clutching a trident, wearing a Corinthian helmet and holding a Greek warrior's oval shield, Frances Stuart, Duchess of Richmond and Lennox, sat as the model. She was a real beauty, famed for rejecting the advances of King Charles II, but it is sadly not known if she had any tattoos.

5 Nailed

 There's nothing to see, not one stone left standing upon another, not even much sign of ground disturbance, and the notice on the gate to beware of the bull tends to discourage closer exploration. And yet on the other side of the fence, under a wide meadow of old pasture, there lies an epic story of victory and defeat, a place where the tide of world history almost washed over Scotland and then receded. It is also a place of several firsts.

Tacitus' account of the glorious culmination of his father-in-law's campaign in Scotland sets his triumph in AD 84 at the Battle of the Graupian Mountain, wherever that is. Gnaeus Julius Agricola (lest he seem too exalted, it should be remembered that his cognomen means 'the farmer', although it is unlikely he had straw in his ears) defeated the host of the Caledonians somewhere in the northeast, perhaps on the slopes of Bennachie, a singular mountain near Inverurie. Like many classical historians, Tacitus put speeches in the mouths of opposing generals before battle is joined. The leader of the opposition was Calgacos, the first Scotsman in history to be given a name. It means something handy, like 'the Swordsman'. In an otherwise terrible television history of Scotland made in the early 1980s, this great warrior was memorably played by Billy Connolly, and not for laughs.

Tacitus had given Billy some good lines, stirring stuff about the Caledonians being the last of the free. Unusually, there turned out to be a grain of truth in the invented rhetoric.

Like all new emperors, Domitian sought to buttress his claim to power with a vivid splash of military success that would play well in Rome, and it was decided that the inclusion of Caledonia in the empire would do nicely. Apart from Tacitus, no one cared that the weather was miserable and the land next to worthless, little more than a windy wilderness of mountain, moorland and savages. The political point was precisely that Caledonia was remote, in the frigid far north. If Rome could conquer it, then what could it not do? The defeat of Calgacos meant that the military reach of the empire was long and that the emperor's power over the known world had no limit.

Agricola led his men south after the battle and, having given it the appropriate name of *Victoria,* had them build a permanent base, what would be a military town, Scotland's first town.

In the early summer of 1961, a team of archaeologists dug an exploratory trench across a small area of what they suspected was a very large Roman fort. Soil discolouration in one area suggested that they might have come across a large pit. It turned out to be very deep, and at its bottom they would eventually find hidden treasure.

Under six feet of gravel, the team at last uncovered the corroded remains of metal wheel tyres, rings of iron made by blacksmiths to fit around wooden cartwheels to prevent them from splitting or being damaged on rough and stony tracks. Under these, something odd came to light. It was a solid crust of rusted iron. This turned out to be a thick, heavy lid, perhaps one that might discourage diggers from going deeper. When it was carefully lifted out, an astonishing find was uncovered.

Well preserved from corrosion was a cache of more than 900,000 Roman nails. All them beaten out on the anvils of legionary blacksmiths, they were precious evidence of a building project conceived on a vast scale. The nails varied in size according to their function: some were small tacks for securing roof tiles to sarking, others spikes between 17 and 25 centimetres (6½ and 10 inches) long that were used to clench load-bearing roof trusses and wall beams, and to drive through the hands and feet of the victims of crucifixion, a characteristically Roman punishment. Nothing like this had ever been found anywhere in the Roman Empire.

Agricola's legionary fortress of Victoria was built on a wide meadow above the banks of the River Tay at Inchtuthil. It was intended to be a home base for about 5,300 soldiers, and it covered 53 acres behind a high rampart and a defensive ditch. Inside were 64 barracks buildings, a headquarters in the centre, 170 storehouses, a large hospital, six granaries, a drill hall and much else. The fort perimeter was 7 miles (11 kilometres) long. Victoria was intended as a military hub that would allow Rome to conquer and to hold Caledonia. Even though there were no upstanding remains, and only faint traces of a few ditches, archaeologists were able to reconstruct perfectly the layout of the whole legionary fortress because, unlike others, the site had never been built on. It was another first, the only place in the entire empire where a complete legionary base had been left undisturbed.

Inchtuthil lies close to the Highland Boundary Fault, and Agricola intended the fortress as the hinge and centerpiece of the first frontier that Rome had fortified. Along what is known as the Gask Ridge, a string of forts lay at the mouths of a series of Highland glens. The strategy was simple. The Romans would never be so foolhardy as to venture into the mountains, territory

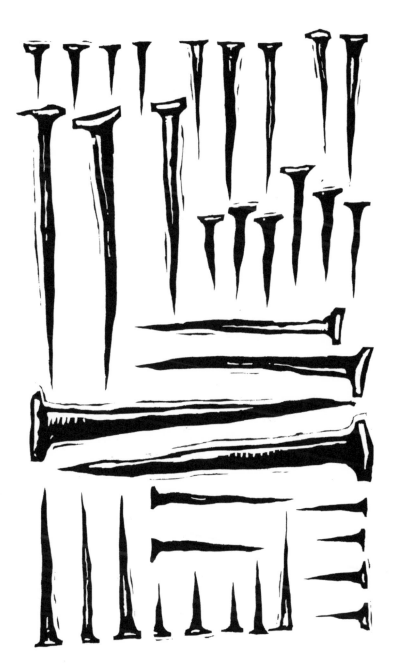

they did not know, perfect for ambush. Instead, they waited for the Caledonians to come to them. If the natives sallied out of their highland fastnesses and moved down the glens to attack and raid the lowlands, then they could be stopped in their tracks by the small army based at Inchtuthil. The Romans understood the geography formed by the terranes, and they exploited it.

The resources needed to build Victoria were staggering, industrial, in their scale. Vast quantities of felled timber were brought to the site, much of it perhaps floated on the Tay, to build the long rampart and the barracks blocks. Clay was dug, puddled and fired to make roof tiles, limestone ground down for mortar and stone transported from a quarry 5 miles (8 kilometres) to the north. A steep gradient led up to the fort, and so the Roman engineers designed a one-way system for laden and unladen ox-carts. A temporary aqueduct brought water in a system of pipework that stretched 2 miles (3¼ kilometres) and the scale of the manual work was huge, involving 6.1 million man-hours.

Then the fortress was demolished. In AD 87, the emperor Domitian ordered that the legion stationed at Chester be transferred to the province of Dacia, modern Romania, where rebellion was flaring on the frontier. With classic Roman ruthlessness and without a moment's hesitation, the Twentieth Legion immediately ceased work at Inchtuthil, demolished the fort, probably setting fire to the timber buildings, and marched south to Chester. Tacitus went in a huff. Having written in glowing terms of his father-in-law's glorious conquest of Caledonia, 'it was straight away let go.' Almost certainly to prevent valuable iron from falling into the hands of native blacksmiths who might beat it into swords and spear tips, the legionaries buried the vast quantity of nails they would have needed to complete the fortress.

This abrupt departure, and the short life of Victoria, appears to have had the effect of erasing all historical memory of this huge enterprise. The only Roman monument to be recognized in the vicinity was a case of mistaken identity. A prehistoric monument known as the Cleaven Dyke, a long embankment with ditches on either side and running arrow-straight for a mile and a half, was thought to be a Roman wall, a much shorter version of Hadrian's. It was as though the fortress had completely disappeared. It may be that as they surveyed the smoking ruins, the native kindreds saw it as a nightmare that had passed. No one in the north had ever seen a settlement on this scale ever before, so many soldiers in one place, and its disappearance must have seemed like a blessing from their gods. Perhaps it had never existed.

The Highlands of Scotland continued to be a concern for Roman emperors, like an itch they couldn't scratch. Hadrian had a wall built to keep the Caledonians and others at bay. Antonine moved it up a bit to link the Clyde with the Forth, and the emperor Septimius Severus crossed the Tweed with 40,000 men at his back, the largest army ever seen in Scotland. None of it worked for long. While in the south, the province of Britannia endured for four centuries, Caledonia was never conquered.

Nor did bribery or acculturation have any effect. The archaeological record of Roman artefacts found in the Highlands is vanishingly scant. North of the Tay there seems to have been little or no contact with the rich province to the south. And yet in the Baltic coastal regions of modern Poland, a very long way from the frontiers of the empire and a place where the legions never set foot, many more Roman coins and artefacts have turned up. The absence of finds in the Highlands might represent a conscious cultural rejection of Rome's so-called civilization, or at the very least an unwillingness to engage with the empire.

Perhaps a simpler conclusion can be reached. A precise historical judgment of the final result of all of that military activity is inescapable: Scotland 1: Rome 0.

And what happened to all those nails? After a few were reserved for display in museums, the rest were sent to Colville's Steelworks to be sorted. Then a brisk retail trade began. Long nails were sold for five shillings and a boxed set of five cost twenty-five shillings. By 1963, all 900,000 had been sold. And so the cache found at Inchtuthil did turn out to be actual treasure. In today's values, their sale raised more than £4 million.

6 Bad Spelling

Over 99 per cent of Scots have difficulty in pronouncing the names of 50 per cent of the geography. North and west of the Highland Boundary Fault the mountains, glens, lochs and straths are named in Gaelic. Less than 1 per cent of Scots speak the language, and its spelling is quirky. Often letters are included in a name that are not pronounced, or pronounced differently, and occasionally entire syllables are ignored.

Most Scots get 'ben' right, but in Gaelic it is rendered as *beinn*, with two more letters than it needs. With something like *Maol Cheann Dearg*, a mountain in Torridon, monoglot English speakers might think they have a chance with something like 'Mole Sheean Deearg'. But they don't. *Maol* is pronounced with a vowel sound not found in English, *Cheann*'s opening consonants are hard, not soft, and *Dearg* is the other way round, correctly pronounced as 'Jerak'. The name means something like 'Bald Red Head'. The surprising thing about the ancient geographers who followed Pytheas is how few mistakes they appear to have made in the earliest maps of Scotland. And most of them never came near the place.

Established in the 3rd century BC by the dynasty of Greek pharaohs who ruled Egypt in the wake of Alexander the Great's conquest, the Great Library of Alexandria was considered one of the wonders of the ancient world. It was in fact part of a larger research institute called the Mouseion, named after the Muses, the nine goddesses of the arts. Despite losing part of its vast collection of scrolled manuscripts in a fire started when Julius Caesar arrived at the mouth of the Nile, chasing Cleopatra and with an army to help him catch her, the library remained an invaluable repository of knowledge for early scholars.

In the middle of the 2nd century AD, it was consulted by a brilliant scholar named Claudius Ptolemy. He drew the earliest surviving map of Scotland. It appeared in the top left-hand corner of his *Geographia*, a much larger map of the known world, essentially the Roman Empire around the shores of the Mediterranean and the lands beyond the imperial borders. The library will have had a copy of Pytheas' *On the Ocean*, and no doubt Ptolemy consulted it. He was especially interested in the readings of latitude (although on the big map he got them slightly wrong), and his *Geographia* also included measurements of longitude. It seems very likely that Ptolemy also consulted another, since lost, account of a circumnavigation of Scotland.

IVS· GERMANI

In his *Agricola,* Tacitus hints that the general ordered the British Fleet, or part of it, to sail around the coasts just as Pytheas had done. It was likely a gesture intended to give the impression of complete conquest. Because there were military imperatives rather than simple curiosity, the naval navigators gathered a great deal of information on the people and their places, and Ptolemy made much use of the log of the voyage in drawing his map. It is a fascinating snapshot, a bright light on early Scotland.

Ptolemy appeared to confirm Tacitus' and Pytheas' observation that Scotland was a patchwork of small kingdoms or kindreds. Some of the names on the map are impossible to parse, but many of them mean something. In Fife, east of the Gask Ridge, lay the lands of the Venicones, the 'Kindred Hounds'. Along the Moray coast Ptolemy plotted the Vacomagi, the 'People of the Plain'. The Lugi in Easter Ross were the 'Raven People', and north of them were the Caereni, the 'Sheep Folk'. The 'Boar Islands' of the Orcades were known to Pytheas, but the Canonacae, the 'Cairn People', on the Atlantic coast make a first appearance in the *Geographia*, as do the Epidii, the 'Horse Folk' of Kintyre. With the latter there exists a remarkable continuity reaching back into the mists of the past. The 'Horse Folk' are still there. The Roman fleet that sailed past the coasts of Argyll had identified the kindred that is now known as Clan MacEacharn. It is one of the very oldest of all the clans, and into the modern period they occupied Kintyre, parts of Islay and Morvern. *Siol Eachairn*, their Gaelic name, means 'Children of the Horse Masters'.

All of these names suggest that animals were totems, a source of identity and perhaps inspiration for these kindreds. Many North American native tribes had similar associations: Mohican warriors sometimes had the turtle tattooed on their bodies, the Crow tribe was known by the English translation of its totem animal and the Cherokee adopted the wolf. The animal names make a further link with the Picts. Salmon, geese, bulls, boars, deer, eagles and wolves all appear on their symbol stones and the like of the warriors of the Lugi might have been tattooed with images of the raven.

The most immediately striking feature of Ptolemy's map is not, however, its detail of Scotland's kindreds. It's the shape. The British archipelago runs broadly on a north–south axis. Most of us live on a 600-mile (965-kilometre) long island. But Ptolemy doesn't draw it like that. Instead, he has bent Scotland through 90°, so that the north coast looks eastwards and appears to be bowing to Europe. Not a good look for some. This extravagant distortion was prompted by Ptolemy's belief that it was impossible for human beings to survive in latitudes north of 63°. If he hadn't bent Scotland abruptly to the east, then the Lugi, the Caereni and others would have been shivering in an impossible 66°. It was a very Mediterranean judgment.

Over the long centuries of copying manuscripts as well as maps, more mistakes crept in. Scribes simply sometimes wrote it down wrong. From nowhere, it seems, an 'r' crept into Aebudae, and the western archipelago forever became the Hebrides. When Tacitus' *Agricola* was first printed in Italy between 1475 and 1480 by Francesco dal Pozzo, one of the typesetters made a mistake. Instead of the Battle of the Graupian Mountain, where Calgacos had made his speech before his army was routed, the printer rendered it as the Grampian Mountain. The name stuck and spread to cover much of the eastern Highland massif.

Before the battle, the kindreds of the north mustered. On his map, Ptolemy noted two places called Coria. It wasn't a repetition. The name means 'hosting-place', where an army gathered before giving battle. These were usually well known and had some cultural and spiritual significance. If the Battle of the Graupian, or Grampian, Mountain was fought on the slopes of Bennachie, as seems highly likely, it may be that Calgacos summoned the kindreds to gather at an ancient stone circle nearby. The second element of East Aquhorthies means 'the prayer field'. Perhaps the gods were implored to give their blessing to the army. If warriors tattooed with their totem animals came, so did the Smertae, the 'blood-smeared people' of the Beauly and Dornoch Firths, and their neighbours the Decantae, the 'Noble Kindred'. Ptolemy's map not only filled in the historical blanks, it sometimes added vivid colour.

For many centuries the Irish were known as the Scots, and the Scots were not called the Scots. Until the early Middle Ages, the memory of the invasions across the North Channel persisted, and for even longer Scots Gaelic was known as Erse or Irish. The name 'Scotland' itself is obscure. It may derive from *sgod*, an old Gaelic word for a sail, a reference to sea raiders or pirates, which is what the first Scots were when they began to attack Argyll. First impressions often stick. The Saxons are so called because they used the *seax* knife, a long dagger that can still be seen on the arms of the old counties of Essex and Middlesex, and the name of the Franks came from their destructive incursions into the Roman Empire. It means 'the Fierce People'.

The Gaelic word for Scotland is *Alba*. Pronounced 'Alapa', it was conferred by the Irish sea raiders and means something like White Land, perhaps a reference to the snow-capped mountains they could see from their ships. The name hangs around in the names of several football clubs founded in the 19th century and in the phrase 'Perfidious Albion', used mostly by the French from the late 18th century onwards. Perhaps they still use it.

Rather than being named after pirates, many Scots might prefer to be thought of as Caledonians, even though the name was originally used by the Romans and others to refer only to the regions above the Highland Boundary Fault. The name is hidden in Dunkeld, the Fort of the Caledonians, and the first element derives from the Gaelic *caled*, which means hard, perhaps rocky or stony. More attractive contrasts with the soft south beckon. Caledonia could just about be interpreted to mean the Land of the Hard Men, and Women.

7 The Problem of the Picts

In a tiny village buried deep in the lush farmland of Angus, not far from the main road between Dundee and Aberdeen, the distant din of an ancient battle can be heard. The thunder of charging cavalry, the roar of war cries, the clash of steel on wooden shields and the screams of dying men echo around a quiet country graveyard.

Standing tall in front of the little parish church is what seems at first like a monumental tombstone. On its long face is carved a ringed Celtic cross. It is intricately decorated with delicately interlaced carvings and flanked by stylized representations of animals wound around serpentine motifs. It is grand, impressive and may indeed be seen as a tomb for a king, a powerful English king. For on the other face of the great stone an extraordinary narrative is carved. It is the story of a battle, one that turned Scotland's history decisively.

In 685, only 6 miles (9½ kilometres) from the little churchyard at Aberlemno, a ferocious battle was fought at Dunnichen. Ecgfrith, king of an expanding and ambitious Northumbria, had ridden deep into the north at the head of a cavalry force, perhaps 500 hundred strong. His ancestors had overrun most of Scotland south of the Forth, and Ecgfrith clearly felt that the tide of history was running with him. His warriors at his back, the Northumbrian king had penetrated far into Pictland, perhaps too far, for when the English reached Dunnichen, they fell into a trap set by Bridei. The Pictish king had signalled for his cavalry to retreat in the face of the enemy advance, luring the Northumbrians into a killing ground from which they could not escape.

The stone tells the story. Arranged in four scenes, it first shows Ecgfrith fleeing, having thrown down his shield and sword. He is pursued by a Pictish cavalryman, perhaps Bridei. The second sequence is a set-piece in which a mounted Northumbrian attacks ranks of well-organized Pictish infantry. Clearly understanding battlefield tactics well, the sculptor shows three ranks: the first man is holding up his shield and he carries a sword, waiting to strike; the second stands directly behind, and pushes his spear past his comrade so that its point can meet oncoming attackers; and in the third rank another warrior waits as a reserve. In the next scene, two cavalrymen are fighting, and in the final act the outcome is made clear. A Northumbrian warrior, probably King Ecgfrith, lies dead on the battlefield, and a crow pecks at his neck.

Had Dunnichen been a Northumbrian victory, Scotland might not exist at all; perhaps we'd call it North Britain. It was a truly pivotal battle, for it preserved a separate identity. The problem is that no one is sure what that identity was.

In 1955, Frederick Wainwright published *The Problem of the Picts*, a book that asked many more questions than it answered. Scholarship has moved on since then, but it remains true that the cultures, languages and peoples of the successor kingdoms of Caledonia are little understood. Hundreds of 'symbol stones', like the one at Aberlemno (and there are two more close by, set up by the side of the B9134), survive, but they resist interpretation. The language has disappeared so completely that no one

can now utter a sentence in Pictish, and there are no written records of the period between the 5th and 10th centuries except the observations of outsiders, and most of them are ill-informed.

Even the name was conferred by others. Sounding very much like a soldier's nickname, the Picts, the 'painted people' (tattooed, more like), were probably first seen from the ramparts of Hadrian's Wall some time near the end of the 3rd century AD. By the 4th, they had worked out how to sail around it, and Pictish *transmarini* raided as far south as London. Indeed, one of the British king Vortigern's fatally flawed motives for inviting the Saxons Hengist and Horsa to come to Kent was to ward off attacks from the pesky Picts.

Before the coming of the Scots, Gaelic-speaking pirates from Ireland, almost all of Scotland north of the Forth–Clyde Line, the old Antonine Wall, was controlled by Pictish kings. Remnants of their lost language survive in place-names (*pit* is characteristic; it means a portion of land, and can be seen in Pitreavie in Fife, Pitlochry in Perthshire and Pittodrie in Aberdeen) that plot the extent of Pictish territory. The enigmatic symbol stones mirror that distribution, with clusters from Fife up the fertile coastal straths to Aberdeenshire, round the corner to Moray and then on up to Caithness. There are also stones on Orkney, Skye and a handful down the Atlantic shore.

When St Maelrubha, St Moluag and others took the word of God into Pictland, its kings embraced the new faith. When Columba came to Iona in the middle of the 6th century, he was gifted the little island of Iona by a local Pictish king. Archaeologists have discovered the remains of a major monastery at Portmahomack in Easter Ross. It was an important centre for copying manuscripts (in Latin, not, sadly, Pictish), stone-carving and metalworking. And in another early Pictish monastery one of the most stunning works of art ever made in Scotland was produced.

One morning in 1833, a gang of gravediggers began work in the ancient cemetery around the ruined cathedral in St Andrews. As they dug deeper, the men came across a series of strange stone fragments. Some were substantial, and when they brushed the earth off one of them, it turned out to be an extraordinary relief sculpture of a man in what looked like a Roman toga killing a lion with his bare hands. The gravediggers had found the St Andrews Sarcophagus. Made in the second half of the 8th century, it was almost certainly commissioned by the most powerful of all Pictish kings. Dying in 761, Oengus, or Onuist, was high king of all Pictland, became overlord of the Gaelic-speaking kindreds in the west and also exerted power over Northumbria. Oengus could fairly claim to be the first king of Scotland.

The sarcophagus is magnificent, influenced by Mediterranean art but unique in its style. It may have been intended as a royal shrine in the church that preceded the medieval cathedral at St Andrews. Oengus reigned for nearly thirty years and was responsible for establishing St Andrew as his kingdom's patron saint. Andrew was a man who knew Christ, and his relics, housed in the church, began to draw pilgrims to his shrine.

Scottish historians used to write about the disappearance of the Picts with a palpable sense of relief. In a bloody battle in 839 in Strathearn, a Pictish army was cut to pieces by a Viking host and many of the nobility were slaughtered. No more symbol stones appeared after around 850, and so that, mercifully, was that. The problem of the Picts may not have been solved, but at least it had gone away.

Or had it? In 2012, geneticists working on Scotland's ancestral DNA came across a new marker. It was given the generic label of 'R1b', the distinctive signal of the first farmers to have come to Britain, the men who had built the halls at Balbridie and Crathes. Research refined the results from a robust sample of 3,000 DNA tests, and they showed something surprising. Relabelled 'R1b, str47-Pict', the marker demonstrated convincingly that the Picts had not disappeared. More than 175,000 Scottish men carry this marker, and there are high concentrations in the old Pictish heartlands of Tayside and Moray. Not only are the Picts alive and well, many of them walk the streets of Dundee and Elgin.

8 The Pirate Kings

 Scotland was never inevitable. There were moments when almost anything seemed possible, like Dunnichen, when our history could have travelled in many different directions. Instead of Scotland, we might now be living in Pictland, speaking a lost language, in Alba, speaking Gaelic, in Norseland, speaking a version of Norwegian, or in northern England. Too often we read history backwards and see a clear path behind us that was always going to lead to now. We invest events with far too much certainty, and that can be a mistake, a misreading. The original derivation for the word 'history' is from the Greek *histor*, meaning 'a witness'. To understand our history better, we should try to think like witnesses, try to grasp how events and the forces that shaped them appeared to people at the time, not looking backwards, knowing what the outcome was. Uncertainty ought to insist on its place as a constant theme. Faced with the prancing squadrons of armoured knights and ranks of deadly Welsh archers at Bannockburn, Robert Bruce probably judged that defeat was the more likely outcome. At Flodden in 1513, James IV believed he would win and charged downhill with a larger army to a terrible defeat, and before Culloden, the Highlanders who faced a government army had never lost a battle.

An alternative version of Scotland began to sail across the North Channel in the 5th and 6th centuries. Only 12 miles (19 kilometres) separates the Northern Irish shore from the Mull of Kintyre, and on clear days sailors have the comfort of navigating by line of sight, always allowing for the surging rip tides that run between the mighty Atlantic and the Irish Sea. Until the coming of the railways in the mid 19th century, water was a more certain and faster means of travel than any land journey, and it is likely that there had been traffic across the North Channel and up and down the coasts for centuries before migration from Ireland to southwestern Scotland began in earnest.

What became known as the kingdom of Dalriada began to coalesce in Argyll. The name derives from *dal*, an Old Irish word for a portion of land and *Riada* or *Reuda*, which seems to have been a personal name belonging to a leader of some kind. He or his predecessors probably led raiding parties to the Scottish coast before beginning to settle. Unusually, a written document survives that fleshes out the size of the population and the internal divisions of Dalriada. The *Senchus Fer na h'Alban* is a muster list of naval forces. It also notes that the kingdom was made up of four kindreds, and notes the territory of each. The people of Gabran held Kintyre, those of Oengus were in Islay and Jura, the kindred of Loairn was around the Firth of Lorne and that of Comgaill was in Cowal and Bute. It seems likely that Dalriada's capital place, where kings were inaugurated, was the singular rock of Dunadd in the Kilmartin Valley.

The Dalriadan kindreds not only carved out their lands from the Picts in the north but also had eastern neighbours to contend with. After the fall of the Roman province of Britannia in the early 5th century, the Old Welsh-speaking kingdom of Strathclyde survived in various forms until the 11th century. Its kings ruled from Dumbarton Rock on the River Clyde and were known as the Britons.

When the spectacular road that runs north along the shores of Loch Lomond begins to climb into the mountains, drivers sometimes notice a huge boulder that seems to balance on a rocky knoll on the western side of Glen Falloch. This is the Clach nam Breatann, the 'Stone of the Britons', and it once marked an ancient frontier. To the west lay the lands of the Scots of Dalriada, and to the north was Pictland, and place-names remember when violence flared. Lomond is from the Old Welsh *llomon* for a beacon; when raiders launched their boats on the waters of Loch Lomond, warning beacons were fired on the slopes of Ben Lomond to alert the kings and their warriors at Dumbarton. The old frontier is remembered by more Gaelic place-names. Another Clach a Breatunnach, Stone of the Britons, stands at the head of Loch Goil, and it is truly massive at 8 metres (26 feet) in height and 10 metres (33 feet) in width. These monoliths were linked by streams and other features in the landscape with the word *criche* attached, the Gaelic word for a frontier. And in the farthest south, the Firth of Clyde was protected from Dalriadan pirates by coastal fortresses on Bute and on the little islands of the Cumbraes. The latter name translates as the 'Isles of the Britons'.

The pirate kings were ambitious, and none more so than Aedan MacGabrain. Between 574 and 603, he led his warband into battle with the Picts and with Rhydderch Hael, king of Strathclyde. Naval expeditions of Dalriadans sailed north to raid Orkney and south to the Isle of Man. But when Aedan ventured east, he suffered a resounding defeat. At Degsastan, at the head of Lauderdale in the Scottish Borders, he met the army of the Northumbrians, led by King Aethelfrith, an ancestor of Ecgfrith.

So badly beaten that he may have been deposed, Aedan faded from history after Degsastan.

In the 6th and 7th centuries, different versions of Scotland seemed to drift in and out of focus. Gaelic-speaking kings from Ireland attacked both Picts and Britons (whose languages were probably mutually intelligible) before being driven back by warriors who roared their war cries in Old English. As power waxed and waned, any one of four outcomes was possible. It took centuries for Scotland's indigenous languages, Pictish and Old Welsh, to die and for Gaelic to triumph in the north and English in the south. It was inevitable that these two cultures would contend, and sometimes it was a close-run thing.

By the 9th century, the descendants of Aedan MacGabrain had begun to claim the kingship of Scotland, or at least Alba, that part north of the Forth–Clyde Line. The most famous was Kenneth MacAlpin, reputedly the first king of Picts and Scots or Gaels, and traditionally the first name on lists of Scotland's kings and queens. From him a line of MacGabrain kings claimed descent, and it seemed that a version of the nation of Scotland began to coalesce around them. In fact, their rights to the throne were vigorously and repeatedly disputed.

While the power and pretension of the MacGabrain dynasty grew, another of the four kindreds listed in the *Senchus Fer na h'Alban* appeared to disappear. After 736, there is no mention of the kindred of Loairn in Argyll. Their kings and warbands had vanished from history.

In fact, they had migrated. Probably under pressure from the neighbouring Picts, the Loairn kindred trekked up the Great Glen and began to settle in Moray. There they grew powerful, and, as one of the original founders of Dalriada, they became rival and credible claimants to the throne of Scotland.

A German chronicle for the year 1040 records that: 'Duncan, the king of Scotland, was killed in the autumn, by his Dux Macbethad, Findlaech's son, who succeeded to the kingship for seventeen years.'

Defamed as a blood-soaked usurper by William Shakespeare, Macbeth was nothing of the kind. Not only was his claim legitimate, he ruled sufficiently well and securely that he was able to go on pilgrimage to Rome, where 'he scattered money like seed'. Shakespeare's play was first performed in 1606, three years after the accession of King James VI of Scotland and I of England and Ireland. The king had spent years in suppressing the power of the Highland clans, and so the playwright, ever mindful of political sensibilities, characterized Macbeth as a savage, uncivilized Highlander; the audiences at the Globe Theatre were meant to breathe a sigh of relief when nice Malcolm III arrived from the south to take over from the beastly tyrant, this wild, lawless, unprincipled monster. And as for his wife...

Despite reigning for longer than most, Macbeth is scarcely acknowledged in the lists of Scottish kings and his successor, Lulach, not at all, even though both claims were legitimate. Lulach was the son of Queen Gruoch, whose family had title to the throne of Alba in their own right.

The kindred of Loairn continued to contend for the throne. In 1085, a man with the fascinating name of Maelschnetai, 'Follower of the Snows', was calling himself king of Moray, and his successor fought hard to depose the kings in the south. It all ended in an act of unspeakable savagery. After another rebellion in 1228 or 1229, King William the Lion sent knights to capture the last living claimant from the house of Loairn. She was a baby and the king's men dashed her brains out against the column of the market cross at Forfar.

While stereotypes were just that, and there was savagery on both sides, it should be remembered that the wild Gaels of the west did bring the word of God to Scotland. From Ireland a succession of holy men – Columba, Brendan, Moluag, Maelrubha and others – settled first in Dalriadan territory before fanning out across Pictland to spread a message of love, piety and forgiveness.

9 English Scotland

'*Oor gan oot the toon tae take the bonnie bairns doon tae splash in the burn*' might have been a sentence uttered by Robert Burns, except that he wrote better sentences, or by any of the poets and authors who use the Scots language. Also known as *Lallans*, a corruption of 'Lowlands', Scots is recognized as the third language of Scotland, and dialects of it are probably spoken by more people than either standard English or Gaelic. When the Scottish Parliament was reconvened in 1999, the highlight of the celebrations was Sheena Wellington singing Burns' 'A Man's a Man for a' That', much of it in Scots.

In fact, the sentence above could just as easily have come out of the mouths of Geordies, the dialect speakers of Tyneside. And in fact, that dialect, very close to Scots in vocabulary and structure, has been spoken on the banks of the Tyne and in Northumberland and Durham for longer than it has in Scotland. Scots is the descendant of Northumbrian English, not the other way around.

After Degsastan in 603, Aethelfrith and his warbands brought the Tweed Valley and the Lothians (and Dumfries and Galloway) into the kingdom of Northumbria. They imposed not only their rule but also their language. Dialects of Old Welsh had been spoken all over Britain since the coming of the Romans and almost certainly long before, and it occasionally peeps out through the undergrowth of history in place-names: Peebles is from *pybyll*, a shieling, Kelso is from Calchvynydd, meaning Chalk Hill, and Penicuik derives from Old Welsh for Cuckoo Hill. Just as the British did throughout their vast empire, conquerors quickly established the primacy of their language. It was in most natives' interest to learn it.

From the early 7th century onwards, the Anglians, the English invaders, brought more than language. Settlements began to resemble southern models, and there is a perfect example in the Scottish Borders. Near Selkirk, the little village of Midlem, originally Middle-ham, has a classic English village green with a smiddy on it. On either side are rows of cottages and behind them are long backlands where villagers grew garden food, perhaps kept a cow and piled up a midden of unmentionables. These strips of cultivated land are now green pasture, but they show up very well in aerial photographs after a dusting of snow.

East Lothian is often cited as the most English of Scotland's old counties, and there is some truth in that assertion. Villages such as Dirleton, complete with their green and small ruined castle, would not look out of place in Dorset or Somerset. History also adds a gloss to the ancient rivalry between Edinburgh and Glasgow. After the stronghold of the castle rock was captured by English warbands in 638, and the nascent town below it was subsumed into the territory of Northumbria, Edinburgh has long been seen as more anglified than Glasgow. The latter might be understood as more Celtic because of recent history: the arrival of many Gaelic-speaking Highlanders evicted during the Clearances of the 18th and 19th centuries, and the waves of Irish immigrants after the Potato Famine of the 1840s.

When motorists on the M8 drive up the watershed slopes of Harthill, halfway between these two historic cities, they are crossing a frontier that in some ways has more meaning than the one at Gretna Green or Berwick-upon-Tweed. And in many important senses, that border between England and Scotland is a distortion, a division of ancient unities.

The Battle of Carham, fought on the banks of the Tweed, almost precisely on the line of the modern border, in 1018, was as decisive and pivotal as Dunnichen in 687 had been. In May of that year, Malcolm II of Scotland had made an alliance with Owain, the last of a long line of kings of Strathclyde. In the woods of the narrow valley of the Caddon Water, near Galashiels, they massed their host for the descent into the old kingdom of Northumbria. Scouts reported that Uhtred, Earl of Bamburgh, had reached the Tweed near Cornhill at the head of a force of spearmen.

On 26 May 1018, two armies faced each other on the flat floodplain near a ford over the river. In the 11th century, battles were fought mainly on foot by forming shield walls that bristled with sword and spear. Having made sure that they could not be outflanked and surrounded, soldiers advanced towards each other, often only at a walk, and battle was joined. Over the top of their long shields, terrified men stared into the eyes of their enemies, only feet apart, as they pushed and hacked at each other. They could smell the sweat, taste the blood and sense the fear. Men often sought courage from alcohol, and the reek of ale and mead would also have been in the air above the river.

Victory was a matter of impetus as much as numbers, and also technique. The phrase 'my right-hand man' is a memory of fighting in a shield wall. Most warriors were right-handed, and when they raised their sword arm to strike a blow, they exposed their ribs to the thrust of a spear or an enemy sword.

The defensive role of the right-hand man was therefore critical, but it also produced another effect. In a shield wall, warriors also pushed their comrades forward, especially if their shields were tight together, 'rim to boss', and this made battle fronts move to the right, wheeling like rugby scrums sometimes do.

Right-hand men have a different supporting role in modern society. Perhaps it is not accidental that the best man at a wedding ceremony traditionally stands to the right of the groom.

On that blood-soaked May morning on the Tweed 1,000 years ago, Malcolm II's army of Gaelic- and Old Welsh-speaking warriors won the day, perhaps by outflanking the Northumbrian spearmen. But it was a hard fight, and King Owain of Strathclyde was probably killed. After 1018, there were no more kings at Dumbarton Rock. For those watching from the ridges above the river, Carham was a disaster, a victory won by foreigners, warriors from the north, outsiders, men who probably spoke different languages. Inclusion in the kingdom of Scotland and removal from England may have felt like the annexation of German-speaking territories on the Rhine by France after the First World War.

God knew no frontiers. But his worshippers did, and that has led to more distortion in both directions. In the 7th century, the greatest native English saint was born, raised and ordained in what is now Scotland. Sources are both blurred and sharp. Cuthbert's name confirms that he was of Anglian stock, and probably high-born. As a shepherd boy in the Border hills, he saw a vision that changed his life. In the eastern sky, Cuthbert watched the soul of St Aidan being carried from the monastery at Lindisfarne up to Heaven in the arms of angels. Inspired by what had been revealed to him, the young man rode (carrying a spear and accompanied by a servant) to the Celtic monastery at Old Melrose in a loop of the Tweed and asked if he might be permitted to take holy orders. Cuthbert rose to become prior of the community, and was later persuaded to go to Lindisfarne to be its bishop.

His exemplary life was the subject of three near-contemporary biographies, and a powerful cult developed around this pious, vulnerable man. Cuthbert was loved, and perhaps England's most spectacular cathedral was raised on his bones. Durham became home to his shrine and many pilgrims came to enrich the great church and its prince-bishops. But despite all these contradictions, this most English of saints should not be thought of as Scottish by birth and upbringing, but as Northumbrian.

Anomalies abound elsewhere. One of the greatest artworks of the early English church is to be found in Scotland. Probably the earliest surviving example of English literature is inscribed on the shaft of an Anglian cross at Ruthwell in Dumfriesshire. Known as the 'Dream of the Rood', the narrative is told by the cross itself as Christ was crucified:

> *I [lifted up] a powerful king,*
> *The Lord of Heaven I dared not tilt.*
> *Men insulted both of us together,*
> *I was drenched with blood poured from the man's side.*

The carving on the Ruthwell Cross is beautiful and was once painted in bright colours, but it is the poem that resonates down the centuries, the beginnings of English literature, to be found in Scotland.

Origins were forgotten and indeed reversed in 1513 in the disastrous battle at Flodden. Holy relics often accompanied medieval armies to encourage soldiers to think that God and his saints fought at their sides. In the midst of the English host flew the scarlet banner of St Cuthbert, carried by the clergy of Durham Cathedral.

But on both sides at Flodden, similar dialects of English rose in the throats of soldiers as they roared their war cries and encouraged their comrades.

10 The Islands of the Strangers

'Immense whirlwinds, flashes of lightning and fiery dragons were seen flying in the air,' wrote the chronicler, and then a great famine followed. These were indeed portents of evil, for when Tuesday 8 June 793 dawned, 'heathen men came and miserably destroyed God's church on Lindisfarne, with plunder and slaughter'. It was an assault that sent shock waves throughout all Christendom, through Britain and Western Europe, an attack on the sacred heart of the Northumbrian kingdom, on the shrine of holy Cuthbert. When news reached Alcuin, a Northumbrian scholar at the court of Charlemagne, he was aghast. 'The church of St Cuthbert is spattered with the blood of the priests of God, stripped of all its furnishing, exposed to the plundering of pagans.'

The Vikings had sailed into history.

When the monks on Lindisfarne climbed up to the Heugh, a rocky outcrop on the southern shore of the island, and looked east, out to the horizon of the North Sea, they saw the sails of the dreki, the dragon-ships. By that time it was too late. As the sea lords roared for their oarsmen to pull hard and their keels rasped up on the shingle beach, the monks ran to bolt the doors of their church. But it was too late. The Vikings raced up the shore, broke into the defenceless monastery, stole the treasures of Cuthbert, gifts brought to his shrine for more than a century, slaughtered the fleeing, bewildered monks and desecrated the holy places with their foul, pagan presence.

Chroniclers wrote that a 'shower of Hell' had burst over Britain. Columba's monastery at Iona was attacked in 795, 802, 806, 807 and 825. Abbot Cellach had no choice but to abandon the island made sacred by the tread of the great saint and generations of pious monks. He moved the community to Kells, inland in Ireland, and there the great gospel begun on Iona was completed – and misnamed the Book of Kells. The monastery at Applecross, founded by St Maelrubha and very influential in the conversion of the Picts, was destroyed so completely that it never recovered. All down the Atlantic shore, in Ireland, the Isle of Man and along Welsh and English coasts, the pagan raiders were merciless. With no regard for sanctity (except for a knowledge of the dates of the Christian festivals, when all the treasures of the church would be on display and easier to seize), they attacked monasteries defended only by God's grace. Part of the shock was that His protection was not enough. Indeed, some monks actually sought martyrdom, perhaps to atone for sins that had prompted God to allow the Vikings to attack and destroy. In 825, Blathmac led a community of monks back to Iona even though he knew that the warriors known as the Sons of Death would come. It seems he believed that red martyrdom, a blood sacrifice, was needed. When the monk refused to tell a raiding party of Vikings the location of what remained of Iona's treasure, they attached ropes to his hands and feet, hitched the other ends to four ponies, slapped their backsides and tore him limb from limb.

As the attacks continued, and perhaps because the supply of church plate and precious objects had begun to dry up or was better hidden, the Vikings sought other valuables. In the

9th century, they colonized Dublin and set up a slave market. 'Thrall' is the Norse word, and it has gone into the language. Slavery grew into a lucrative business for the sea lords, and many merchants began to come to the market to buy. The appetite for Christian slaves in the courts of the Caliphs and their Emirs in Moslem Spain acquired an even crueler twist, as captive men were sometimes gelded to make them more manageable and attractive to buyers.

By the middle of the 9th century, the raiders had begun to settle. Norwegian Vikings almost completely erased native Pictish identity on Shetland and Orkney. On the Isle of Lewis and on Harris, place-names and clan names remember the Viking takeover. Stornoway, Steornabhaigh in Gaelic, derives from the Norse Stjornavagr, which means 'steering bay'. Mountainous

Harris, Na Hearadh, is from the Norse for 'high land'. Some other names are functional. Cape Wrath, the farthest north-western point of the Scottish mainland, has nothing to do with anger. It too comes from Norse, and basically means 'turn left'.

Clans thought to be quintessentially of the Celtic Highlands and Islands turn out to derive from Norse name-fathers. The MacIvers were originally the Sons of Ivar, the MacAuleys the Sons of Olaf, the MacAskills the Sons of Askell and the MacLeods the Sons of Ljotr. The most powerful clan of the Isles in the medieval period, the MacDonalds, are also sometimes known as Clan Ranald, or the Sons of Rognvald. By the 11th century, the Hebrides had also become part of the Norse kingdom of Man and the Isles, and they were known as the Innse Gall, the 'Islands of the Strangers'. The name stuck and is still used.

Viking incursions drove the kings of Dalriada from the west coast and over the mountains into what is now Perthshire and Angus. The relics of St Columba, contained in the Brecbennach, the reliquary that was carried by the Scots into the Battle of Bannockburn, were translated for safety to Dunkeld. But by the early 13th century, the descendants of the Dalriadan kings had begun to push back. In 1262, Alexander III, King of Scots, offered to buy the Islands of the Strangers, but was rebuffed. Instead, King Haakon of Norway mustered his fleet in a place that remembers the billowing sails and ranks of oarsmen. Between the mainland and the Isle of Skye there is a sheltered anchorage still known as Kyle Akin, 'the Straits of Haakon'. The sight of the 120-strong fleet bobbing at anchor off the shores of Loch Alsh, their war colours flying in the breeze, must have been an awesome sight.

Haakon and his sea lords unfurled their sails and, making headway through the straits at Kylerhea, set a course to the south for the Firth of Clyde and the heart of Lowland Scotland. But the Norwegian fleet was scattered by a storm and badly damaged before fetching up onshore at Largs, where an indecisive battle was fought. What really turned events was the death of Haakon two months later. The Scots attacked Caithness and Skye in 1264, and then forced a deal on the Norwegians. The terms of the Treaty of Perth signed by Alexander III of Scotland and Magnus VI of Norway in 1266 awarded Haakon's successors 4,000 marks a year in return for giving up the overlordship of the Hebrides and the Isle of Man.

Shetland and Orkney remained in Norwegian hands until 1468, when another deal was done – but never completed. It was arranged that James III of Scotland should marry Margaret, daughter of Christian I of Denmark and Norway. As part of the princess' dowry, the Danes pledged Orkney and Shetland to the Scottish crown, but actual sovereignty was never formally transferred. That means something simple and surprising. Technically, the Northern Isles still belong to Denmark's royal family, because their kings and queens have never renounced the right to redeem that pledge.

Culturally, Shetland and Orkney remained distinct for much longer. Until the 18th century, Norn, Scotland's fifth language, was spoken there. A dialect of Norse, its cadences can still be heard in the English spoken in Lerwick on Shetland and Kirkwall in Orkney. Fishermen are superstitious, and many who sail out of the ports of the islands still use some words of Norn; *drolti* for cod, *knoklin* for mussels and *da glyed* for halibut. Some philologists believe that, especially in Shetlandic English, they can still hear the Vikings talking.

Students of ancestral DNA have discovered a persistent phenomenon. Scottish men who seek to find out the origins of their ancestors almost always hope to be a descendant of the Vikings. Most sensible people would run a mile at the sight of the sail of a dragon-ship on the horizon, but for some unfocused, probably macho, reason, these ferocious raiders have retained a dark allure.

11 The Lost Cities

Once the worst of the winter has passed, crowds flock to the point-to-point racing run by the local hunts in the Scottish Borders. One of the most well-known courses runs in a wide circle on the old pasture of a broad river peninsula bounded by the River Tweed on two sides and the River Teviot on the third. Known as Friarshaugh, it is popular with spectators because in the middle of the peninsula there is a small knoll that allows the crowd to see most of the races. Only in one place do the horses and their jockeys disappear for a moment. Near the Teviot, they seem suddenly to run down into a dip before reappearing to race around a wide bend.

Few of those cheering on the horses they've backed realize that they are standing on the site of a lost city, what was once the capital place of Scotland in the 12th century, with two churches, a grammar school and a royal mint, and great markets that drew merchants from Europe. On the little hill in the middle of the racecourse stood the town of Roxburgh, where urban life in Scotland began. Now, nothing of it can be seen, no trace whatever, not one stone left standing upon another. The only hint of its existence is the dip where the horses and riders momentarily disappear. It was the ditch below the town's walls.

Across the Tweed stand the majestic ruins of Kelso Abbey, and in its cartulary, the collection of medieval documents that detailed the lands and rights owned by the monks, the watermark of the lost city can be clearly made out. There were three main streets: the Headgate, or Senedegate, King's Street and Market Street. Near the banks of the Tweed, where a long, straight stretch of the racecourse runs, stood St James' Church, and in the centre of the town there was another, called Holy Sepulchre. The name of Friarshaugh is a memory of a Franciscan friary that stood near a ford over the Teviot. The monks at Kelso Abbey ran a grammar school in the town, but perhaps the most significant building was a royal mint.

Coins were needed because trade was expanding rapidly. Roxburgh first comes on written record in 1113, when Earl David (later to become King David I) brought French monks to found a monastery in the Borders. By the middle of the 12th century there were four major abbeys in Scotland, at Kelso, Melrose, Jedburgh and Dryburgh. The son of the saintly Margaret, David I was a pious king, but he also had a clear eye for business. The abbeys soon built up huge estates and used their imported expertise to exploit them. All had extensive sheep ranches in the Cheviot and Lammermuir Hills; the abbot of Melrose managed lands that supported 12,000 ewes and rams.

Roxburgh became the commercial hub for a brisk and expanding trade in wool and hides. It was protected by a mighty royal castle built on a long, steep ridge at the narrow, western neck of the river peninsula. Recognizing that the town was the main commercial hub of his kingdom, David I spent a great deal of time at Roxburgh Castle, and many documents were issued *apud Rokesburgum*, as his clerks stamped them with the royal seal.

While the town flourished as the wool trade expanded dramatically, the castle was not new. An ancient stronghold, strategically placed, it bore an old name. Marchidun is from Old Welsh and it means the Horse Fort, or the Cavalry Fort. Across the Teviot, traces of a Roman road appear to have been identified, and many coins picked up by metal detectorists. Most date to the 4th century AD, right to the very end of Roman Britain. There exists credible, if circumstantial, evidence that in the early Dark Ages, when Britain was forming, a charismatic cavalry leader may have been based at Marchidun. His name might have been Arthur.

What stimulated the growth of Roxburgh was the export trade. In Flanders, in the cities of Bruges, Ghent and Ypres, textile manufacture had become semi-industrialized by the 12th century. The high-quality woollen cloth turned out by Flemish weavers was in demand all over Western Europe, and local supplies of wool were insufficient to meet it. Merchants travelled a long way to come to the market at Roxburgh, and each year lucrative deals were done in Market Street with the monks of the Border Abbeys and their agents. For the times, the trade was on a huge scale. In 1296, the abbey of Melrose alone sold 2,000 fleeces and 3,000 sacks of wool. These reached the port at Bruges through Scotland's second lost city.

Berwick-upon-Tweed has not disappeared, but it has been lost to Scotland and is now a forlorn outpost, by far the northernmost town in England, a place politically and economically disconnected from its natural hinterland.

The wool and hides bought at Roxburgh market were probably floated down the Tweed on rafts or riverboats. When these cargoes reached the quays at Berwick, they were loaded onto ships for the North Sea passage to the port at Bruges.

In the Scottish town, the Flemings established the Red Hall, and German merchants were to be found at the White Hall. These buildings are lost now, but they probably resembled the 'factories' of British traders in colonial India, storehouses where a measure of diplomatic immunity was permitted. In Roxburgh, there may have been a Black Hall, but no nationality was attached to it.

The ships from Flanders that tied up at Berwick's quays brought both everyday goods and luxuries. Wine was by far the biggest import, since it was needed for the many masses said and sung each week in the abbeys and other churches, and it was no doubt also enjoyed by those prelates and nobles who could afford it. Iron, timber, cauldrons, metal pans, dyestuffs, alum, basil, garlic, ginger, pepper, rice, almonds and sugar as well as many other useful and exotic items were brought from Europe and even further afield. The customs and other taxes paid at Berwick made the town wealthy, and very important to Scottish kings. In 1286, the revenues from the import and export trade was £2,190, compared with £8,800 for the whole of England.

War destroyed this vibrant economy. Having overcome the Welsh princes, Edward I of England seized the opportunity offered by dynastic failure in Scotland. From the 1290s onwards, more than two centuries of intermittent cross-border warfare disrupted wool production and the markets where it was sold, and finally disconnected Berwick from Scotland. By the 15th century, Roxburgh, too, had begun to disappear. The castle had been 'doung to the ground' so that English invaders could not occupy it, and without its protection, and with the severance of trade through Berwick, the town withered and died. Its wooden buildings rotted and sank into the grass, while stone robbers from Kelso and elsewhere helped themselves.

If history had turned in another direction, it could all have been so different. The Tweed Valley and its lost cities were the commercial centre of Scotland in the 12th and 13th centuries, but dynastic politics made the region marginal, a border land.

12 Fatal Attraction

In the great hall of Edinburgh Castle, the logs on the fire blazed and crackled, long tables groaned with food and wine flowed as servants replenished goblets and cups. It was the night of 18 March 1286, and King Alexander III was carousing with his cronies. Each man sat not with a plate in front of him but a tranche, a thick slice of rough bread on which he put whatever meat, fish or vegetable he lifted from great platters. Hearty eaters were known as trencher men. That night the king sent a dish of lampreys over to one of his barons, telling him it was Judgment Day. 'Then my lord,' the nobleman roared as he piled these eel-like fish onto his tranche, 'we shall all rise again with full bellies!'

Outside in the darkness a late winter storm was raging, blowing down the Firth of Forth off the sea, whipping white spindrift off the waves and whistling around Edinburgh Castle's high rock. As more wine was drunk, the roaring in the great hall grew loud and perhaps bawdy. Suddenly King Alexander rose from the table and announced that he needed female company. Now! That very night! He would lie with his new queen, the beautiful, twenty-one-year-old Yolande de Dreux. The king was forty-four, but by God he could still mount a woman and father children on her.

Having been a widower for ten years, Alexander had acquired a reputation as an enthusiastic womanizer, not above forcing his intentions, even on nuns, it was alleged. His son and heir, also Alexander, was growing up, so there was no dynastic need to re-marry, and it seems that this king saw himself a merry widower. But then, at the age of twenty, the prince died and an heir was urgently needed. No doubt the king's cronies roared their approval and encouragement when he announced that he would bed his new queen. The stability of the kingdom depended on royal ardour.

The only impediment, all that stood in the way of the king's wine-fuelled passion, was that Queen Yolande was not in her chamber at Edinburgh Castle. She was spending a night with her attendants at the royal manor of Kinghorn, on the far shore of the Firth of Forth.

A great deal is known about the events of 18 March 1286 (except for the precise date, which might have been the 19th), for they were recorded by the chronicler at Lanercost Priory. Near Carlisle, lying close to the line of Hadrian's Wall, the canons at Lanercost were very well informed about events in Scotland.

When it became clear that King Alexander was serious, that he would indeed ride through the darkness and the winter storm to the ferry on the southern bank of the Forth, the more sober of his barons tried to dissuade him. But 'neither would he be deterred by the stress of weather nor yield to the persuasion of his nobles, but straight away hurried along the road to Queensferry.' Ostlers in the royal stables saddled horses, and with only three esquires to escort him, the king clattered across the cobbles, out of the gate of Edinburgh Castle and into the raging night.

It was black-dark when they reached the ferry, and the boatman refused to make the crossing. It was too dangerous in

the roiling sea and the stinging wind. 'Are you afraid to die with me?' said Alexander. Perhaps when gold and silver coins glinted in the flicker of torchlight, the ferry boat was made ready. Despite the stormy weather, the king and his escort gained the safety of the northern shore.

When he scrambled onto the jetty, Alexander was met by someone who knew him. At that time the master of the salt-pans at North Queensferry, Alexander le Saucier had previously been a cook in the royal kitchens. It is striking how directly, and without a shred of deference, he made his views clear. 'My lord, what are you doing out in such weather and darkness? How many times have I tried to persuade you that midnight travelling will do you no good?'

But the king's passion was not dampened by the driving rain, the midnight darkness and the roaring wind. Having asked le Saucier for local guides, Alexander III made his way along the cliff path. It seems that in the murk, he became detached from his escort. Perhaps their shouts could not be heard above the howling blast. Horses hate these conditions. As flight animals, they are deprived of their hearing, and the king's mount may well have spooked, lost its footing or missed a turn in the path. At Pettycur, where there is a near-sheer drop to the sea, Alexander's horse fell, plunging him over the cliffs to his death, and plunging Scotland into two centuries of warfare with England.

On the clear morning after the storm, searchers found the king's body on the beach. His neck had been broken. The survival of the long-reigning MacMalcolm dynasty, kings who had given Scotland stability, now depended on a little girl who lived on the other side of the North Sea, the Maid of Norway.

Only three years old in 1286, Princess Margaret was Alexander's granddaughter, and on his death she became queen-designate. A council of Guardians of the Realm of Scotland was appointed, but Edward I of England quickly intervened, insisting that the little girl be betrothed to his son, Edward of Caernarvon, the future Edward II. In 1290, the Treaty of Birgham was agreed. It stated that Scotland would remain fully independent despite the marriage, but quite how that would work in practice was unhelpfully unclear and in any case, Edward I would soon ignore it. There were also grumblings and murmurings among the Guardians. The Bruces and Balliols both believed that they had strong claims to the throne in the event of the death of Margaret.

And die she did. In September 1290, the Maid of Norway's ship made landfall on Orkney. She became ill. Perhaps from food poisoning, compounded by sea-sickness, the princess expired in the arms of the Bishop of Bergen. Having endured for centuries, the MacMalcolm dynasty had at last failed.

Centuries of chaos followed, the consequence of too much wine on a winter's night in Edinburgh.

13 Wallace, Moray and Bruce

 On 10 July 1296, a crowd of soldiers, noblemen and prelates gathered at the market cross at Stracathro, a village near Brechin, halfway between Aberdeen and Dundee. The king of Scotland was dragged into their midst and made to stand before Edward I, king of England. In a deliberately humiliating ceremony, John Balliol had his knightly girdle removed, his surcoat, blazoned with the royal lion of Scotland, ripped off and the royal signet ring pulled from his finger. Then the symbol of his authority, the royal seal, was smashed on the cobbles. No doubt to a roar of laughter from his barons, Edward I is said to have remarked, 'A man does good business when he rids himself of a turd.'

Chosen as king of Scotland by Edward in 1292, in the wake of Princess Margaret's early death, John Balliol had led an unsuccessful rebellion and, after his ritual shaming, he abdicated and was carted off to prison in the Tower of London. Much worse fates awaited those who had supported and followed him. Nevertheless, resentment at England's attempts at colonization burned bright.

William Wallace came out of nowhere. A minor lord from Ayrshire, his name derived from the Old English *Wylisc*, meaning 'Welshman'. In times not so long past, it seems that Wallace's family spoke Old Welsh, the language of the ancient kingdom of Strathclyde. Mel Gibson had other ideas. In *Braveheart*, a very well-made Hollywood action film, he gave the hero a Glaswegian accent. At least the future site of the city lay within the bounds of the old kingdom.

Whatever he sounded like, Wallace was a gifted leader. When rebellion flared after his murder of William de Heselrig, the English sheriff of Lanarkshire, he rode to Glasgow to gain the support of Bishop Robert Wishart and the Scottish Church. At the same time, Andrew Moray raised the standard of resistance in the north when he seized Inverness Castle and was joined by rebels from Aberdeenshire. Messengers rode back and forth and the two forces joined. The Lanercost chronicler was not

impressed, writing of 'a certain bloody man, William Wallace, who had formerly been a chief of brigands in Scotland, to revolt against the king and assemble the people in his support.'

Careful to style themselves as Guardians of the Realm, Wallace and Moray acted on behalf of King John, thus giving themselves constitutional legitimacy. Only four months after the murder of de Heselrig, a huge English army marched north to confront the rebels at Stirling. Its general, Hugh de Cressingham, had two devastating weapons at his disposal: in open field the charge of his armoured knights was irresistible, especially after the ranks of the enemy had been thinned by volleys of arrows from Welsh archers.

But neither came into play. Because of incompetent English leadership, complacency and the courage of the Scots, a battle at Stirling Bridge was won. When the English knights and infantry began to cross the only bridge over the Forth, Wallace and Moray allowed them to pass. But not all of them. When as many soldiers as they felt they could deal with had crossed, or as the chronicler Walter of Guisborough wrote, 'as many of the enemy had come over as they believed they could overcome', the Scots rushed from the flanks to cut off the end of the narrow bridge, isolating de Cressingham and many of his knights on their side of the Forth. Wallace and Moray's spearmen surrounded the reduced English army and cut them to pieces. In the circle of death, many were pulled off their horses and slaughtered, including their general.

Success was short-lived. Andrew Moray was mortally wounded at Stirling Bridge, and Edward I himself came north to deal with William Wallace, who promptly made a catastrophic tactical misjudgment. Just as the English army was running out of supplies and about to retreat south, the Scots offered battle in open field. Edward I gave thanks: 'As God lives ... they need not pursue me, for I shall meet them this day.'

After defeat at Falkirk, support for William Wallace faltered badly, and in 1305 he was betrayed, captured and taken south to suffer the appalling death of a traitor. Stripped naked and tied upside-down on a hurdle pulled by a horse, he was dragged through the crowded streets of London. Refuse and worse was thrown at him, and as they did with other victims, those leading the horse may have stopped so that men in the crowd could urinate on Wallace's face. On the scaffold at Smithfield he was butchered. Having been hung by the neck until almost unconscious, Wallace was tied to an upright hurdle so that the baying crowd could see what the executioner would do to him.

First he cut off Wallace's genitals and, to cheers, held up the bloody handful. Then he and others began to disembowel the prisoner. Skilled men with very sharp and specially made knives aimed to keep their victims from going into shock, so that they could see their entrails burning on a brazier while they still lived. Only then came the merciful release of the block and the headsman's axe.

Despite these dreadful and widely publicized cruelties, the rebellion in Scotland continued. John Balliol had abdicated, and, unlike Wallace, Robert Bruce had a genuine claim to the throne of Scotland. In 1306, he was crowned in an ancient ceremony at Scone Abbey near Perth. His wife, Elizabeth, was not hopeful: 'I am afraid, my lord, that we have been made King and Queen, as boys are made in summer games.'

But events began to turn. A year later, Edward I led another vast army up the western route from England to Burgh-by-Sands, near Carlisle. They camped on the salt marshes on the southern shore as they waited for low tide so that they could wade and ride across the Solway Firth. The landward western passage between England and Scotland was then a wide area of treacherous bog, and much the safer and wetter option was to splash across the firth, following the line-of-sight markers on the farther shore, making sure not to stray into the deeps. But before his soldiers began to cross, Edward I died. He was sixty-eight, very old for the times. His army turned back, and Bruce was given a respite and some good fortune.

Edward II possessed physical courage, it was said, but lacked the leadership qualities of his father. When at last he assembled an invasion force in 1314, there was a constant rumble of dissent and dissatisfaction among the major magnates. And the English king made the great mistake of allowing the Scots to choose the battleground. Such a large army was bound to come north on the only good road, one built by the Roman legions more than 1,000 years before. It led to Bannockburn, and to destiny. For the Scots, the early portents were good.

When the English vanguard saw Robert Bruce's battalion on the edge of a wooded area known as the New Park, near Stirling, hotheadedness immediately trumped common sense. Sir Henry de Bohun thought he could make out a mounted figure in front of the ranks of Scottish spearmen. Was that Bruce? Was that a gold circlet around his helmet? Adrenalin pumped as de Bohun saw a chance for glory, a chance to kill the usurper and win the coming battle with a single death. Digging in his spurs, kicking his war-horse into the gallop, he couched his lance and charged.

Bruce may have had his back to de Bohun, for his spearmen roared for him to retreat behind their ranks. But the king did not hear them. With only moments to react as the Englishman levelled his lance, his war-horse racing across the grass, Bruce waited until he was almost upon him. As the point of the lance searched for the king's breast, he suddenly neck-reined his little pony to the offside, not allowing de Bohun time to swing his lance over his horse's head. As the knight passed, Bruce stood up high in the stirrups and with his axe struck a mighty blow to de Bohun's head, killing him instantly.

Much bucked by their king's bravery, the Scottish spearmen joined battle with a vastly superior army on the following day and defeated them. Because the Earl of Gloucester led a charge of armoured knights too soon and in too restricted a space, his archers could not fire for fear of killing their own men. But it was sheer determination that won the day. In the murderous ruck of hacking, jabbing, pushing and shoving of close-quarter battle, there often came a tipping point, and that is what happened at Bannockburn. When, almost imperceptibly, some in the English ranks began to take a step backwards, the Scots roared, 'On them! On them! They fail!' As many as 10,000 Englishmen died, and the legend of a hero-king was born.

Bannockburn is important to Scotland's sense of herself. It is the narrative of the unofficial national anthem, 'Flower of Scotland', but it also symbolizes a sensible reality. England may be ten times larger and much more powerful, but sometimes the little guy wins.

14 Smarter Scots

 Superstitious students at St Andrews University sometimes perform a strange sidestep when they walk down North Street. Set into the cobbles outside St Salvator's Tower and its 15th-century chapel and quadrangle are the initials PH. They stand for Patrick Hamilton, a member of St Leonard's College who began to preach the heretical precepts of Martin Luther in 1523. Hearing that he was to be tried for heresy, he fled, but on his return to St Andrews in 1528, he was arrested, tried and condemned to be burned at the stake on the same day.

Outside the chapel, soldiers began to build the young man's pyre. No doubt watched by a crowd, he was led out in his sark and chained to a stake to be burned alive. Most who suffered this dreadful fate were quickly asphyxiated by the smoke from the fires that roasted their feet and legs. But it was a dank February day, and a wind blew up North Street, fanning the flames but blowing the merciful smoke away. Hamilton spent six hours in unspeakable agony before the flames finally reached his chest and head.

Most St Andrews students know only that this man was martyred, and they avoid stepping on the PH out of respect, and also to avoid bad luck in their exams. But they are aware of

history. After Oxford (founded in 1096) and Cambridge (1209), St Andrews is the third oldest university in the English-speaking world. And in Scotland it was not alone for long. After its foundation in 1413, St Andrews was joined by four other universities. Glasgow was founded in 1451, King's College Aberdeen in 1495, Edinburgh in 1583 and Marischal College in Aberdeen in 1593. For centuries, the English rubbed along with only two universities while Scotland had five until the Aberdeen colleges merged in 1860.

St Andrews received a papal bull of foundation so early because Bishop Wardlaw was good at playing off one pope against another. The medieval Church saw several schisms, and in the early 15th century there were popes in both Rome and Avignon. Scotland supported the latter, Benedict XIII, while England was in the camp of the Roman pope. Wardlaw argued that to keep Scotland's loyalty, the Avignon pope should agree to the establishment of a university. Other Scottish bishops began to make similar advances, and papal bulls were granted to Glasgow and Aberdeen. Edinburgh was founded as a post-Reformation college. The first new English university to be added to the Oxbridge duopoly was Manchester in 1824.

Scotland's long tradition of university education became part of the nation's identity. At first, the ancient colleges mainly turned out graduates in divinity and the law, but the curriculum did expand. By 1740, Edinburgh had the pre-eminent medical school in Europe.

Scotland was also the first country in the world to embark on a programme of mass literacy (see Chapter 16), and since the five ancient universities were local and familiar to most people, and not so expensive as Oxford or Cambridge, a slightly wider range of students attended. Most of the great figures of the

Scottish Enlightenment in the second half of the 18th and the first half of the 19th centuries were either professors or associated with the universities. In 1869, seven women matriculated in medicine at Edinburgh University, and by 1892 all of the Scottish universities admitted women.

The most profound widening of access came in 1963 with the publication of the Robbins Report. It persuaded the government to offer maintenance grants to students, essentially making university education free and accessible to all who could pass the exams. But it was a brief window. From the 1980s, Conservative governments began to close it again and now a university education is very expensive and essentially unavailable to those who cannot afford it. It is a tragic waste of Scotland's greatest resource, its people.

Historians should try to be objective, but here I must pause to declare a deep personal interest. As a beneficiary of the provisions of the Robbins Report, I graduated in history from St Andrews University in 1972. Having been elected Lord Rector in 2011 by the students, I returned to chair the university court for three years. My term of office coincided with the 600th anniversary of Bishop Wardlaw receiving the papal bull, and I was immensely proud to walk, behind my mace-bearer, at the head of celebratory processions. These had a distinctly medieval atmosphere as I followed in the footsteps of my predecessors as the 48th Rector.

15 Whaur's Yer Wullie Shakespeare Noo?

Sir, I wald spear at yow ane question
Behauld sum Prelats of this Regioun:
Manifestlie during their lustie lyvfis,
Thay swyfe Ladies, Madinis and uther mens wyfis.
And sa their cunts they have in consuetude.
Quidder say ye that law is evill or gude.

One word jumps out of this passage of 16th-century Scottish literature, but two others perhaps need translation. 'Swyfe' probably means screw, in a sexual sense, and 'consuetude' is an antique word meaning a custom that had legal force in Scotland. Elsewhere in this remarkable text, what might be the earliest use of the word 'fuck' occurs in its modern spelling and meaning.

All of this and much, much more appears in the pages of *Ane Pleasant Satyre of the Thrie Estaitis.* It is a verse-play written in the middle of the 16th century by Sir David Lyndsay of the Mount, a laird from Fife who became Lyon King of Arms at the royal court, and also a diplomat. An interlude from the play was performed at Linlithgow Palace in 1540, with King James V and his courtiers in the audience. The first full-length version was probably staged out of doors at Cupar in Fife in 1552, on a playing field below the Castle Hill. The audience needed stamina and strong bladders, for the actors took the stage at 9 o'clock in the morning and the closing scenes did not take place until 6 o'clock in the evening.

The Three Estates, as it is now styled, was a remarkable play, and not just for its length, the use of profanity and other bawdry. It was a sustained satirical attack on the institutions of 16th-century Scotland, much of it played for laughs in front of the king. The three estates of the Scottish Parliament were the clergy, the nobility and the burgesses from the towns. None escape the sharpness of Lyndsay's pen, but as in the passage above, the clergy were attacked especially mercilessly. Precisely at the time the play was being performed, Catholicism was tottering in Scotland, and the abuses and hypocrisies of some of the characters in *The Three Estates* might almost be seen as historical documents. Only eight years after the marathon performance at Cupar, the Reformation Parliament swept away the Catholic Church and its libidinous prelates.

Using the Scots language, the vernacular, rather than Latin, the play is significant in at least two other senses. It might be seen as one of the first literary expressions of Renaissance values and thinking in Scotland, a mixture of sophistication and coarseness. Lyndsay knew how to make his audience laugh. But more than that, *The Three Estates* is startlingly outspoken. No group of powerful people, including the king in the audience, was beyond its reach. One wonders at the playwright's role and status. As Lyon King of Arms, Lyndsay was in charge of ceremonial at court as well as being a member of the parliament he lambasts, and yet he was given licence to do much more than simply poke fun. Very near the surface of the text of the play is powerful, withering criticism.

At the second Edinburgh Festival in 1948, the first modern production of *The Three Estates* was staged in the Church of

Scotland Assembly Hall. Much cut by Robert Kemp, with all fucks and cunts removed, and starring the gifted comedian and actor Stanley Baxter, it was a great success. There have been regular revivals. In 1996, John McGrath adapted Lyndsay's play, and in it Sylvester McCoy, a future Dr Who, played it for laughs, and got them.

One of the most interesting aspects of *The Three Estates* is the use of coarse language, for it shows how that has changed over time. Five centuries ago, religious swear words were probably much more frowned upon than the sexual sort. Now, little offence is caused by 'for Christ's sake', 'Damn!' and the like. In Melissa Mohr's *Holy Shit: A Brief History of Swearing*, she makes the point about the changing fashions of swear words: 'When they lose power, it's just those taboos getting weaker, and new ones coming in to replace them.'

16 The Chapel

In the deep, sunless canyon of Edinburgh's Cowgate there stands a half-forgotten cradle of Scotland's history. The Magdalen Chapel was built as an alms-house in 1541, but less than twenty years later it was at the centre of a revolution. With a crenellated roof-line, large stained-glass windows and a square tower for a spire, it looks more like a small church than a refuge for the poor and homeless. It is now little noticed, overshadowed by the bustle and traffic of George IV Bridge, rising high above.

History was made behind the chapel's doors. In 1560, it housed the first General Assembly of the Church of Scotland. In August of that epoch-making year, the Scottish Parliament had abolished Catholicism, made the mass illegal and established the Reformed Church as the national Church. Compared with events in England and Europe, it was a relatively bloodless revolution. There were a handful of martyrs, like Patrick Hamilton, who died horrific deaths, but there was little or no general per-secution. As the ministers of the new Church, many of them former priests, packed into the Magdalen Chapel, the voice of John Knox was heard.

Modern portrayals and perceptions of this great man see him as a joyless ranter, hectoring the beautiful, vulnerable Mary,

Queen of Scots, and converting the colourful public life of Scotland into a grey, dour, devout nation. It is difficult to imagine a more unfair or inaccurate assessment. Knox was one of the founders of modern Scotland, and with others he did much that was positive to shape contemporary society.

In the Magdalen Chapel, the General Assembly appointed a commission headed by John Knox to write the new Church's constitution, and by a quirk of fate, his colleagues in this great endeavor were John Winram, John Row, John Spottiswoode, John Willock and John Douglas, all sharing the same Christian name. Between them, the Six Johns compiled what was known as the *First Book of Discipline*. Its guiding principle was to reverse the direction of Church governance. Instead of a top-down administration where the Vatican appointed bishops and told them what to do, and bishops controlled priests and their parishes, the congregations of Scotland were given the right to elect their ministers. This change was of enormous importance, since the minister was a vital individual in every city, town and village. And it was a very different approach from that of the Church of England, where vicars were appointed by bishops, often on the recommendation of the gentry and the aristocracy.

Working at high speed in the chapel, the Six Johns organized the *Book of Discipline* into nine heads, or chapters. In all of them, it was made clear that authority ascended from the congregation and gave them, the elders and the deacons a motive part in the life of the new Church and therefore in society. This was a decisive cultural shift, a limited version of democracy, and in stark contrast to how the Reformation was adopted south of the border.

Education was seen as crucial to the Reformed Church in Scotland, what became known as the Kirk. Martin Luther and

Jean Calvin promoted the doctrine of the priesthood of all believers. Instead of depending on the mumbo jumbo of Catholicism, where the mass was said in Latin and therefore inaccessible to most communicants and priests were seen as intermediaries who alone spoke to God, the reformers believed that each individual ought to be responsible for their own salvation. That in turn required everyone to be able to read the Bible, the sacred Word of God, for themselves. Which, of course, required literacy. The *Book of Discipline* pronounced that, 'seeing that God hath determined that His Kirk here in earth shall be taught not by angels but by men, and seeing that men are born ignorant of God and all Godliness', wealthy people should pay for the education of their children, while 'the children of the poor must be supported and sustained by the charge of the Kirk.'

In other writings, John Knox insisted that every parish was to have a school and a schoolmaster to 'teach grammar and the Latin tongue'. He went on: 'Further, we think it expedient that in every notable town there be erected a college, in which the arts, at least logic and rhetoric, together with the tongues [languages], be read by sufficient masters for whom honest stipends must be appointed.'

The immediate difficulty that the Kirk had in this great, civilizing enterprise was that it had to deal with the greed of well-connected lairds and even burgesses. As the monasteries were dissolved, the great estates of the likes of Kelso and Melrose were broken up and much of the land claimed by local grandees. The wide estates of the dukes of Roxburgh are made up of much of the patrimony of Kelso Abbey, including its sheep ranches in the Cheviots. The Crown also grabbed its share. As a consequence, the new Church was impoverished from its beginnings, and it took centuries for Knox's dreams to be realized. After the feverish activity in the Magdalen Chapel, literacy became common, but only by the later 18th and early 19th centuries. In the counties of Caithness and Berwickshire, at either end of Scotland, between 70 and 77 per cent of people could read and write. This was Knox's great achievement, yet it is often forgotten, as the image of the beetle-browed killjoy overshadows the reality.

In some measure, this widespread impression of the man came about through comparison. When Mary, Queen of Scots arrived in Scotland from France (where her husband, King Francis II, ruled for little more than eighteen months before his early death) in 1561, she was set on a collision course with Knox and the reformers. Though a committed Catholic, she recognized that her realm was now Protestant, but when Knox preached against her, condemning the glamorous young queen for hearing mass, dressing too elaborately and dancing, sparks flew. Mary summoned her critic into her presence, and showed real acuity in their debate. But when she attempted to have Knox condemned for treason, no jury would dare to convict him, such was his popular support.

It was the contrast between a young, beautiful and vivacious queen and the grim, dogmatic Knox that distorted his image and impaired his legacy. He was a truly great, visionary Scotsman and should be revered and remembered with gratitude.

17 Robert Carey's Ride

In the winter of 1602/3, Elizabeth I of England began to die. Almost seventy, a great age for the times, she had reigned for forty-five years, but when the winter winds whistled around Richmond Palace, Gloriana, the great queen, was fading. She appeared to have fallen into a deep depression. Several of her life-long friends and advisors had recently died, and courtiers remembered that she mourned them deeply. Not leaving her chamber, Elizabeth stood at the window in silence for long periods. Her ladies set cushions on the floor in case she fell or sank down. But sometimes her famous temper still flared. When her chief minister, Robert Cecil, told the queen that she must go to bed, she snapped 'Must is not a word to use to princes, little man!'

Perhaps Elizabeth stood because if she lay down during the day, she feared she might never rise again. For some time she had refused most food and sipped only a little liquid. It was said that the queen became emaciated, that she had a very thick layer of white makeup on her face, had lost all of her teeth and most of her hair, and refused to be bathed. The old lady must have been a ghoulish sight. But there was one matter that had to be resolved before death took her, something vital she had to communicate.

Maybe she had thought it a sign of weakness, of waning authority, but Elizabeth had never explicitly named her successor. Most believed that it had to be James VI of Scotland. He was the queen's closest male living relative, and both were direct descendants of Henry VII of England. Robert Cecil had opened secret negotiations with the Scottish king, and his regular letters to Elizabeth had been well received by her.

Four days before she died, the queen lost the power of speech, possibly after a minor stroke. When close to death, she was asked if James VI should succeed, and it was said that she made a circle around her head to signify a crown.

Between 2 and 3 o'clock in the morning of 24 March 1603, Elizabeth I of England at last died, and an extraordinary plan

went immediately into action. Despite being expressly forbidden by the royal council, Robert Carey had prepared meticulously. At regular stages along the Great North Road to Edinburgh, he had organized changes of horses so that he could cover the long journey without stopping. When word came to Carey that the old queen was near to death, he stole into Richmond Palace and waited in the courtyard, under one of the royal bedchamber's windows. When the breath went out of Elizabeth's frail body and her eyes were closed, one of her attendant ladies pulled off her finger a ring with a blue stone. Philadelphia Carey then went across to the window, opened it, called to her brother and threw down the ring. It had been a gift from James VI of Scotland, and when Carey arrived in Edinburgh he would give it to the king,

along with the news he had been waiting for all his life. The ring would prove that the old queen was dead, and James would become the first king of Great Britain and Ireland. And as the bearer of this momentous news, Robert Carey would surely be richly rewarded.

Having managed to escape from Richmond Palace, this messenger of destiny rode like the wind for Scotland. Far faster than any official dispatch, Carey arrived in Berwick-upon-Tweed only forty-eight hours after leaving London. Somewhere near the town, his horse spooked in the darkness, threw its rider and kicked him in the head while he lay on the ground. Blood- and mud-spattered, Carey eventually clattered into the inner courtyard of Holyrood Palace in the early hours of 26 March. Despite his appearance, he convinced the guards to wake their royal master. When the king asked the muddy and wet messenger what letters he carried from the Privy Council, Carey replied that he had nothing except 'a blue ring from a fair lady'. James took it, and said, 'It is enough.'

Eleven days later, the new king of Great Britain and Ireland sat on a dyke near Musselburgh, waiting for traffic travelling in the opposite direction to pass. It was the funeral cortege of Robert Seton, Earl of Winton. He had been one of the group of noblemen who had rescued the king's mother, Mary, Queen of Scots, from captivity, and a life-long supporter of the Stuart dynasty. Out of respect and affection, James VI and I took off his hat, bowed his head and waited as the mourners passed.

'I desire a perfect union of laws and persons and such a naturalizing as may make one body of both kingdoms under me, your king,' said the new monarch to the Houses of Commons and Lords who crowded into Westminster Hall. A union of the crowns was to be much more than dynastic; James was determined to weld England and Scotland into one nation as well as a united kingdom.

The English were not keen, and in Scotland, God was against it.

James wanted Cumberland, Northumberland, Berwickshire, Roxburgh and Dumfriesshire to be known as the Middle Shires. There was to be a common currency based on a 20-shilling piece called a 'Unite'. An Instrument of Parliamentary Union was formulated, the separate legal systems were to be made uniform and all Scots born before 1603 would become naturalized English subjects. In the time-honoured fashion, a time-wasting device was proposed by English MPs. A commission to 'perfect' James' programme of reforms was set up. And nothing happened.

James VI and I also made difficulties for himself. Openly bisexual, he shamelessly played favourites, something that mattered because these young men had not only the king's ear but also often controlled access to him. Having fallen in love with George Villiers, the handsome son of a minor Leicestershire knight, the king promoted him first to be Earl and then Duke of Buckingham. Their correspondence was very explicit, and James called Villiers his wife and himself the young man's husband. A surviving letter from the young man includes this account: 'Whether you loved me now ... better than at the time which I shall never forget at Farnham where the bed's head could not be found between the master and his dog.'

The Church of Scotland no doubt disapproved, but its leading ministers were far more concerned that the king's plans for political union might submerge the newly formed Kirk into a Church of Great Britain dominated by the bishops of England. The Scottish reformer Andrew Melville had annoyed the king in 1590 by reminding him that in Christ's kingdom of Scotland, he was not a king, nor a lord, nor a head, but a member. In England, it was different, and until his death in 1625 James was every inch a commanding king, both publicly and privately.

Robert Carey's plan backfired. At first he was made a Gentleman of the Bedchamber, but when James reached England and listened to criticism from his councillors, he summarily dismissed Carey from royal service.

18 The Chosen People

 On 23 July 1637, during a Sunday service at the High Kirk of St Giles in Edinburgh, a stool flew through the air. It was the first in a series of incendiary events that led directly to a scaffold being built outside the Banqueting House in London.

The stool was aimed at the head of James Hannay, the Dean of St Giles, who had begun to read from the new *Book of Common Prayer*. High Anglican in tone, imposed by Archbishop Laud with the enthusiastic support of Charles I on a deeply Presbyterian nation, it was a spark that ignited a great conflagration. 'Dare you say mass in my lug!' roared Jenny Geddes, as Dean Hannay ducked. After her outburst, the service turned into a riot, and the clergy were fortunate to escape with their lives.

By October of the same year, Scotland had become dangerously unstable, and rebellion flickered in the febrile air. In what amounted to a *coup d'etat* against the king, the Five Tables was set up. Essentially this was a parliament with five estates of noblemen, lairds, burgesses, ministers of the Kirk and an executive committee. Instead of negotiating, Charles I issued a proclamation that demanded obedience. Sparks were fanned into flames, and in 1638 the Five Tables met at Greyfriars Kirk in Edinburgh and promulgated a document that set Scotland – and England – alight.

The National Covenant stated that Christ and not the king was the head of the Church of Scotland, and it made Charles I's kingship conditional on his maintaining Presbyterianism in Scotland. It was, in effect, a declaration of war. The Covenant was made between God and the people of His realm of Scotland, the chosen people. Those who met at Greyfriars were clearly confident that God agreed with them, and was not just at their side but their leader.

Copies of the Covenant were sent all over Scotland for signature and also, crucially, to those Scots serving in Europe as mercenaries. Alexander Leslie, who had been made a Field Marshall by King Gustavus Adolphus of Sweden after fighting for him in the bloody Thirty Years War, organized his men to gather in Germany and sign the Covenant. More than that, he persuaded the Swedes to release 300 battle-hardened Scottish officers and 1,000 of their countrymen into his service. Their arrears of pay were made up not of cash, but of new muskets and artillery. With his small army, Leslie landed in Scotland in the spring of 1638, and suddenly the political and military landscape changed.

The Army of the Covenant was swiftly professionalized as Leslie stiffened the ranks of volunteers with his mercenary officers and soldiers. Local lairds were often made captains of companies, but beside them were lieutenants who had fought in Europe and knew their business. As flags fluttered, bearing the motto 'For Christ's Crown and Covenant', a token uniform was created. To distinguish them from the enemy, Leslie's soldiers wore blue ribbons on their bonnets and blue sashes for the officers. It became the colour of militant Protestantism, and can still be seen on the football pitches of Britain.

With only a show of force from their spectacular camp on the summit of Duns Law in Berwickshire and without striking a blow, the Army of the Covenant brought royalist negotiators to the table at last. But no agreement could be reached in the face of the king's continuing intransigence. And so, in 1640, Leslie led his army, now 20,000 strong, south, scattered a much smaller royalist force at Newburn and took the city of Newcastle. It was the first action in what came to be miscalled the English Civil War.

By 1642, relations between Charles I and Parliament had soured to such a degree that the king left London and raised the royal standard at Nottingham. There followed a year of inconclusive campaigning, and the English Parliamentary party decided to seek the help of the Scots and Alexander Leslie's crack troops. So desperate were they that their commissioners agreed to the Covenanter's demands that England adopt their brand of Presbyterianism. The Calvinist Church of Scotland was to become the Calvinist Church of Great Britain and Ireland.

In January 1644, the Army of the Covenant marched to York to join forces with the Parliamentary party's troops. Because the Scots formed the largest contingent, Alexander Leslie became commander in chief. He also knew what he was doing. In the early evening at Marston Moor, he saw through the telescope he had brought from Holland that the royalists were standing down and beginning to light cooking fires. He immediately ordered an all-out attack on the army, led by the dashing Prince Rupert. Under Leslie's direction, Oliver Cromwell led a division of cavalry that distinguished itself in this sprawling battle. Defeat for the Crown meant that Charles I had lost the support of the largely royalist north of England. After further defeats at Naseby and Langport in 1645, the king was forced to concede that he had lost the war. But rather than negotiate with Cromwell and the English Parliamentary leadership, he surrendered to the Army of the Covenant at their fortress at Newark, near Nottingham.

For six months, Charles prevaricated and procrastinated, refusing to sign the National Covenant and rejecting peace proposals to end the civil war. By the end of 1646, the Scots had had enough of the king, and, being led and staffed by mercenaries who knew how to strike a bargain, they sold him to the English for £200,000.

In January 1649, Charles Stuart, 'that Man of Blood', stepped through the middle window on the first floor of the Banqueting House in Whitehall and onto a scaffold. Wearing two plain white shirts so that the crowd would not see him shiver from the winter cold and think it was cowardice, he asked for his silk nightcap. He wished to tuck his long hair into it so that the executioner's axe could make a clean cut. The block was deliberately and humiliatingly set so low that the king could not kneel, but had to prostrate himself. Before laying his head on the block, Charles spoke to the executioner, and in return for a coin agreed that he would give a signal for the axe to fall. It was a single blow. The axeman quickly picked up the king's head by the hair, and threw it into the crowd.

19 **17007**

In the first half of the 18th century, two English spies helped turn Scotland's history in a different direction.

In October, 1706, Daniel Defoe found lodgings on the fifth floor of Moubray House on Edinburgh's High Street. He had been sent north by Queen Anne's chief minister, Robert Harley, to act as his eyes and ears in Scotland, to be a spy. Negotiations were under way to bring into being an Act of Union between England and Scotland, but the proposal was not popular. From the safety of his eyrie at the top of Moubray House (which still stands, next to John Knox House), Defoe watched in terror as the Edinburgh mob gathered in the street below.

'I had not been long there but I heard a great noise, and looking out I saw a terrible multitude coming up the High Street with a drum at the head of them shouting and swearing and crying out all Scotland will stand together, no union, no union, English dogs and the like ... I cannot say to you that I had no apprehensions ... particularly when part of this mob fell upon a gentleman who had discretion little enough to say something that displeased them just under my window ... a Scots rabble is the worst of its kind ... I was warned that night that I should take care of myself.'

The notion of union made every sort of economic sense for Scotland. The 1690s had seen a series of failed harvests in one of the worst periods of the Little Ice Age. There had been extreme cold and persistent rain. Famine was everywhere, and in 1698 reports of people lying dead on the roads were common. A quarter of the population of Aberdeenshire starved to death. Financial ruin also stalked the land. A vast sum, £150,000, perhaps a quarter of Scotland's disposable capital, was lost in the Darien scheme, an attempt to establish a Scottish colony on the Isthmus of Panama to facilitate trade with the east.

But as often in matters of national identity, heart ruled head, and the Act of Union was deeply unpopular with ordinary people. Although Daniel Defoe was sometimes terrified as well as given to panic, he did manage to gain the trust of both camps. 'Tis the easiest thing in the world,' he wrote, 'to hire people here to betray their friends. In short, money will do anything.'

Defoe reported regularly to Robert Harley, and made only one real misjudgment. Surprisingly, he had managed to infiltrate groups of Jacobite sympathizers. Queen Anne was the last of the Stuart dynasty, and it seemed that, like Elizabeth I, she would die childless. The crown would then pass to the safely Protestant House of Hanover, even though the legitimate claim and court of James VIII and III was in exile in France. Defoe wrote that Jacobites proposed military action, 'but they found themselves too weak for the attempt'. That may have been true in Edinburgh, but in the Highlands there was still strong support and, among many clans, a real will to fight. There were rebellions in 1708, 1715, 1719 and then in 1745.

On 16 January 1707, the Scottish Parliament finally passed the Act of Union, and was thereby immediately dissolved. It was what one member called 'the end of an old song'. But that was not the moment when Great Britain came into being. That happened on the afternoon of 6 March, when the bill was presented to the Westminster Parliament. Alongside measures to better prevent escapes from the Fleet and Queen's Bench prisons and two bills to allow road repairs in Bedfordshire and Hereford-shire, the proposed act was waved through.

After his covert operation in Edinburgh, Defoe found fame elsewhere. He had heard stories of Alexander Selkirk, a Scottish sailor who had spent more than four years alone on the uninhab-ited Pacific island of Juan Fernández, 400 miles (645 kilometres) west of Chile. He survived by hunting and gathering, like his pre-historic ancestors. Selkirk's biggest problem was repeated attacks by aggressive rats while he slept in his shelter. The resourceful castaway managed to domesticate feral cats and they protected him. When Selkirk finally came home to Lower Largo in Fife, local people called him the Man Who Taught Cats to Dance because of his rapport with the animals. Defoe ignored the rats, and for what is generally regarded as the first novel in English literature, he added Man Friday and a band of visiting cannibals. Robinson Crusoe was published in 1719, and has never been out of print since.

The creation of fiction is an essential part of any spy's set of skills, and Dudley Bradstreet was, like Defoe, an excellent liar. After a brilliant campaign in Scotland, Prince Charles, son of James VII and III, and his Highland army had invaded England in the early winter of 1745. When they reached Derby, only 120 miles (195 kilometres) from London, there was panic in the capital. Those who had somewhere else, anywhere else, to go were frantically packing their portable possessions. 'Terror struck in the minds [of people],' wrote a diarist, and there was a run on the banks as queues formed and cash was hurriedly withdrawn.

Bradstreet was travelling in the opposite direction, towards Derby. Somehow, he managed to gain access to Prince Charles' war council, and he warned them that government armies were circling. At Lichfield, only 25 miles (40 kilometres) to the south-west, the Duke of Cumberland commanded 9,000 infantry and a squadron of cavalry. The Duke of Richmond was bringing another army from the east, and Generals Hawley and Ligonier were waiting north of London with at least 8,000 or 9,000 men.

Most of this was pure fiction. Only Cumberland was in the field, and he could have been avoided, and at Finchley Moor in London there had been an unenthusiastic muster of perhaps 3,000 volunteers. The Prince and Cameron of Locheil, chief of the bravest and most feared clan, wanted to press on regardless, but other commanders dissented. No help had arrived from France, and there had been little support in England as the Highlanders marched south. The argument was finely balanced, and it may well be that Dudley Bradstreet's lies were determinant.

Whatiffery is an idle pursuit for historians, but it seems likely that if Prince Charles and Cameron of Locheil had won the debate, the clans would have been led down Whitehall by their pipers as Londoners cowered behind their doors, and the Stuarts would have found themselves once more in St James Palace instead of driven into permanent exile.

20 Frankenstein

On Wednesday 4 November 1818, the corpse of Matthew Clydesdale, a freshly hanged convicted murderer, was made to come briefly alive in a lecture room at Glasgow University. Andrew Ure, a professor and a product of the Scottish Enlightenment, attached electrodes to the corpse that made his chest heave, his eyes open and enabled him to walk a few steps. The experiment was halted by Dr James Jeffery, who plunged a scalpel into Clydesdale's jugular vein, executing him a second time. This was the bizarre culmination of years of medical experiment and by no means an unusual incident in the intellectual ferment of 18th- and early 19th-century Scotland.

John Amyatt was an English chemist who visited Edinburgh some time in the 1770s, and was dazzled by the intellectual life of the city. 'Edinburgh enjoyed a noble privilege not possessed by any other city in Europe,' he wrote. Amyatt was not making a reference to its spectacular location or the long views. 'Here I stand at what is called the Cross of Edinburgh [in the High Street] and can in a few minutes, take fifty men of genius by the hand.'

Amyatt was not exaggerating. It had taken more than 150 years, but the commitment of John Knox and the reformers to education was beginning to bear fruit. By the early 18th century, most Scottish children had access to some degree of education and clever boys (only boys), known as 'lads o' pairts', could go on to one of the country's five universities. With the departure of politicians, placemen and aristocrats to London, Scotland's remaining independent institutions began to flourish, especially the universities. Edinburgh also became a centre for publishing and printing. By the later 18th century, there were sixteen printer-publishers supplied by twelve paper mills.

As John Amyatt quickly discovered, the city was small, and so concentrated that great scholars, philosophers, mathematicians, poets and painters met each other often. Edinburgh was essentially a city of a single street. What is now known as the Royal Mile runs from the gates of the castle downhill to Holyrood Palace. Off this spinal street were 337 closes or alleyways where high tenements housed a densely packed population.

John Amyatt was much taken with the printer-publisher William Smellie. From his premises at Anchor Close, off the High Street, he embarked on a great enterprise in 1768, what he called the *Encyclopaedia Britannica*. It was an age when it was thought possible to capture all human knowledge and record it. Over a hundred weekly installments, the great encyclopaedia rumbled through the alphabet. Some of its entries wasted little time. 'Woman' was four words long, summed up as 'the female of man'. So there.

Drinking clubs as well as publishing fuelled the sense of intellectual ferment. One of the first was the Easy Club, founded in 1712 by Thomas Ruddiman, a printer-publisher. Bubbling cauldrons of debate, and no doubt gossip, these groups met regularly and controversy was stoked. Ruddiman attacked the legacy of George Buchanan, the tutor of Mary, Queen of Scots and James VI, disagreeing with the favourable estimates of and observations on his historical writings. The Select Society was formed 'to vindicate that incomparably learned and pious author from the calumnies of Mr Thomas Ruddiman.' With more than a hint of tongues planted firmly in cheeks, the members of the new club defended Buchanan vigorously. They were Adam Smith, David Hume, William Robertson and the founder, the gifted painter, Allan Ramsay.

Hume was one of the giants of what came to be called the Scottish Enlightenment. The son of a farming family of slender means in Berwickshire, David Home anglicized the spelling of his surname and when he arrived in the city he tried hard to purge what he called 'Scotticisms' from his Borders accent. But he failed to find preferment at either Edinburgh or Glasgow universities, and instead sustained himself mostly by his writing. His *History of England* made Hume famous, but it was his earlier *Treatise on Human Nature* that established him as a brilliant, innovative thinker. Published in 1739, it was in part motivated by his personal struggles (one of his therapies for what sounded like depression was the daily consumption of a pint of claret) as it set out reasons to believe that it was desire rather than logic that governed the behaviour of human beings. Ideas, he argued, were not innate and people only had real knowledge of things they directly experienced. Ethics were therefore not based on a set of moral principles, but on feelings. Hume's work was enormously influential on figures such as Albert Einstein and Immanuel Kant, and the great German philosopher Arthur Schopenhauer wrote that 'there is more to be learned from each page of David Hume than from the collected works of Hegel, Herbart and Schleiermacher taken together.'

Hume's fellow member of the Select Society, Adam Smith, also came from humble beginnings. Raised by his widowed

RAMSAY

HUME

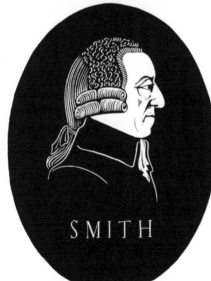

SMITH

ROBERTSON

mother, he attended the burgh school of Kirkcaldy and when he was only fourteen went to Glasgow University on a scholarship. Smith then made the mistake of going south, finding that 'In the University of Oxford, the greater part of the public professors have, for these many years, given up altogether even the pretence of teaching.'

In 1750, Adam Smith and David Hume formed a close friendship. More successful at finding paid employment, Smith had been given a chair in logic and metaphysics at the University of Edinburgh. His lectures formed the basis of his *Theory of Moral Sentiments*, published in 1759. Its central thesis was that human beings' sense of morality was based on what he called sympathy, and we might recognize as empathy. In 1766, Smith returned to Kirkcaldy to spend ten years working on his *Inquiry into the Nature and Causes of the Wealth of Nations*. It laid the foundations of the study of economics and showed how the interaction of mutual self-interest and competition can lead to prosperity. Politicians in particular have interpreted Smith to suit wherever they stand on the spectrum, from right to left. Best to let him speak for himself. Here is his famous dictum: 'It is not from the benevolence of the butcher, the brewer, or the baker, that we expect our dinner, but from their regard to their own interest. We address ourselves not to their humanity but to their self-love, and never talk to them of our own necessities but of their advantages.'

This extract, much quoted by those on the right wing of politics, is often interpreted as intellectual backing for their positions, a succinct statement of the operation of selfishness. But in fact, Adam Smith would not have recognized such an interpretation. Here is the first sentence of his *Theory of Moral Sentiments*: 'However selfish man may be supposed, there are evidently some principles in his nature, which interest him in the fortunes of others, and render their happiness necessary to him, though they derive nothing from it except the pleasure of seeing it.'

So while it might be assumed by some that people are innately selfish, Smith argues that experience suggests otherwise. People derive pleasure from seeing the happiness of others because human beings are social creatures: we care about others and their condition can give us pleasure or pain. It is only through our senses, through putting ourselves in their shoes, what Smith calls empathy, that we acquire knowledge of their sentiments.

Few men in the history of any nation, great or small, can claim to have changed the way people think about the world, but David Hume and Adam Smith did.

21 The Brilliant Blacksmith

Another Scotsman changed the way the Western world looked. The Scottish Enlightenment was not only a revolution of ideas. At the same time as Adam Smith sat at his desk writing about the wealth of nations, James Small was in his smiddy increasing it. In the 1760s, this little-known and half-forgotten Berwickshire blacksmith redesigned the old Scots plough, and changed the landscape.

For many centuries, fields had been ploughed very inefficiently. The old plough, a heavy wooden wedge dragged through the ground by the brute force of at least four beasts, usually a team of plodding oxen, was slow, and when it hit a big stone, it often broke down. The problem was the ploughshare. Made from wood tipped with iron, it was canted to one side, like a wedge, but the surface was flat. Consequently, what was known as the mouldboard did not turn over the furrow-slice completely. This meant that plough-followers were needed to walk behind it, bashing down big clods with mallets and pulling out the weeds.

The old Scots plough was very labour-intensive. Yoked together, the team of oxen had to be led and encouraged by a goadman. When the ploughman holding the stilts could not keep the mouldboard in the ground because of stones or hardpan, someone, usually a child, had to sit on the beam to keep it down. And there were at least two plough-followers behind.

As a blacksmith, James Small often had to repair broken ploughs, and knew well how inefficient it was. But he had an idea, one that would start an agricultural revolution. With the help and encouragement of wealthy backers, he built a bigger smiddy at Blackadder Mount. The wide forge and its big chimney can still be seen in a ruinous building by the side of a B-road in Berwickshire. After making many prototypes and testing them to destruction, Small came close to bankruptcy. But finally he came up with a two-part answer. Instead of the wedge, the flat mouldboard, Small designed a new, screwed shape, exactly like modern ploughs, that would turn over the furrow-slice completely. Not only would this dispense with the need for plough-followers, it also buried the weeds completely, turning them into a mulch for the soil.

The second part of the answer to the problem of the old Scots plough was to make the ploughshare all in iron. Only a year before Small began work in his new smiddy, a much bigger one opened near Falkirk. On the banks of the River Carron, a blast furnace was built that used iron ore from Bo'ness and the techniques pioneered by Abraham Darby of Coalbrookdale. Using coke instead of coal to achieve higher temperatures, the Carron Ironworks began to turn out cannon for the armed services as well as parts for James Watt's steam engine in 1765. By 1814, it was the largest iron works in Europe.

Once James Small had satisfied himself with the new, screwed design, having beat it out on his own anvil at Blackadder Mount, he took the prototype to Falkirk. After more work on the gauge of the iron needed to do the job (the slimmer the better), it was agreed that the Carron Ironworks would turn out the new ploughshare.

Small himself was a skilled ploughman, and attached each prototype to a plough and harnessed beasts to pull it. Once he had perfected the new design, he found that the effect was revolutionary. Because it was all cast in iron in the characteristic screwed shape, the ploughshare sliced through the ground like a knife through butter instead of a blunt instrument. There was much less resistance and that meant that only two (and eventually one) big horses were needed to pull it. This had two very important effects. Ox-teams were not only slow, but also needed a lot of space to turn at the end of each furrow. Medieval fields seen by aerial photography have furrows with a characteristic S-shape caused by the wide turn made by yoked teams of four or even six beasts in heavy soil. Horses are much neater on their feet, more manoeuvrable and responsive to the reins. That meant a much tighter turn was possible at the end of the furrow, bringing more land into cultivation.

The depth to which Small's plough (known as the swing plough when it became common) could delve also made a significant difference. The deeper furrows encouraged better drainage and that also increased the acreage that could be cultivated and planted.

The look of the land also changed over time because of James Small's genius. The ox-teams' difficulty in turning had encouraged farmers to plough in long rigs, often with inefficient drainage ditches on either side. The use of the swing plough and its tight turns altered the shape of fields, encouraged hedging and fencing and even the planting of trees to give shelter.

In the valley of the River Clyde, the dukes of Hamilton began to address the problem of traction. Needing heavy horses whose muscles were better attuned to pulling heavy carts than hunting or jumping, the Hamiltons imported big Flemish stallions to breed with local mares. Their family estates included much of the Lanarkshire coalfield and carts needed to be hauled along waggonways. What became the Clydesdale breed was also found to be very trainable and usually placid, an excellent plough horse. When one was harnessed to the other, fields and farms became more productive.

James Small did not patent his design for reasons that are not entirely clear, and he died in 1793, penniless and exhausted.

The swing plough was widely and quickly adopted at the same time as the Clydesdale breed began to proliferate. Both were exported all over the world, and one historian has commented that without the genius of James Small, the great American and Canadian prairies would have waited much longer to become the bread baskets of growing nations. Few now remember the brilliant – and selfless – Berwickshire blacksmith, but he did change the world.

22 The Man in Tights

In 1822, at a royal levee at Holyrood Palace, King George IV made a spectacular entrance. Swathed from head to foot in tartan, wearing two belts (to restrain his belly – he tipped the scales at 20 stone), dirks and a bonnet, his kilt sat well above the knee over flesh-coloured tights, essential to hide his varicose veins. On the first state visit since the Jacobite Rebellion in 1745, he was in Edinburgh for only a week. Watching his entrance was Lady Dalrymple. 'Since he is here for such a short time,' she sniffed, 'it is as well we see so much of him.' The 'King's Jaunt' was stage-managed by Sir Walter Scott, and it saw the beginning of the wholesale adoption of Highland iconography by all Scots.

Which is very surprising. Only sixty years before, the Highlands and Highlanders had been the victims of repressive legislation that attempted to break the power of the clans – and succeeded. Not only had there been a concerted campaign of genocide and clearance after Culloden, acts of Parliament banning the wearing of tartan and the playing of the pipes were put in place and lasted until 1782. And yet here was a portly king swathed in the stuff, strathspeying, reeling and no doubt sweating around the halls of Holyrood Palace. Something had changed.

Very different stories were being told. In place of the Highlands as a trackless resort of treacherous savages, of warlike clans speaking a different language, of a people intent on bringing down the British state, romance began to swirl around the bens and the glens. In 1760, James MacPherson published what he claimed were *Fragments of Ancient Poetry Collected in the Highlands of Scotland*. Translated into English, these purported to be the first written versions of very old oral compositions collected from seannachies, clan bards. A year later, the mountain mists cleared again, and more of MacPherson's alleged discoveries came to light with the publication of the *Works of Ossian*, a lost epic on the tales of Fingal, a great Celtic hero who suddenly emerged from obscurity. A cave on the island of Staffa was named after him, and Felix Mendelssohn was moved to write a famous overture.

MacPherson's translations were a publishing sensation, bestsellers that enjoyed widespread success across Britain and Europe. Johann Wolfgang von Goethe admired them, and it was said that copies never left Napoleon Bonaparte's side. Others were not so sure. Dr Samuel Johnson dismissed the poems as romantic invention, but that mattered less than their impact. Far to the north of Britain, a world away from the belching chimney stacks and fiery forges of the industrial revolution, there was a land where heroes had walked and where mighty deeds had been done. The romance of the Highlands was born.

Walter Scott stoked the flames of fakery. As the real and present history of the Highlands was ignored, a dismal tale of repression and departure, Scott offered a different version in his novel, *Waverley*. Subtitled *'Tis Sixty Years Since*, a reference to Culloden, it was the first true historical novel. Mixing fiction in the shape of its hero, Edward Waverley, with real characters like Prince Charles (who had become Bonnie instead of dangerous),

it recast the events of the Jacobite Rebellion in the glow of noble sentiment, and with some humour. Like MacPherson's work, *Waverley* was an international bestseller, but on an even bigger scale, and it made Walter Scott the most famous Scotsman who had ever lived. That was the reason he was invited to stage-manage the 'King's Jaunt', the royal visit to Scotland in 1822, and why he clothed it all in tartan.

Other forces were at work. In 1815, the Highland Society of London, by definition a club where sentiment always trumped reality, wrote to each of the clan chiefs asking for a swatch of their clan tartan so that it could be classified and registered. Most had no idea that any such thing existed. In a near-contemporary painting of the Highland charge at Culloden, clansmen are shown wearing a kilt of one sett and a jacket or plaid of another, and no two men are dressed the same. One historian has counted twenty-three different setts. This attempt at classification developed such momentum that more literary fakery was cobbled together to support it. Two brothers by the name of John and Charles Edward Sobieski-Stuart produced what they claimed was an ancient list of clan tartans called the *Vestiarum Scoticum.* It was all hokum, no one ever saw a copy, but none of that mattered either. People wanted to believe. In the 19th century monarchs set fashion trends, and if the king wore a kilt, then so did the rest of high society, and even the middle classes. The textile mills of the Borders thrummed with good business, grateful to Walter Scott, as their looms turned out thousands of bolts of tartan.

The looms have never stopped, even though tartan is now woven all over the world. So successful was Scott's staging of the 'King's Jaunt', and so completely did Queen Victoria fall in love with the Highlands (amazingly, she once said that at heart she was a Jacobite), that Scotland was transformed. A wholesale hijack of the iconography of the clans, tartan, bagpipes, haggis and whisky, took place, and now all Scotland is defined by it. No wedding north of the Cheviots can take place without the groom, the best man and most of the male guests turning up in full Highland fig.

And yet, a little over 200 years ago, no Lowlander would have been seen dead in a kilt. Certainly not Robert Burns. If Walter Scott was the Lowlander who wrote about the Highlands, Burns was the bard of the majority of Scots, those who lived south of the Highland Boundary Fault. In a brief life he was extraordinarily prolific and his vast body of poetry and song lyrics have also been defining. Burns Night, celebrated on 25 January, is a cultural phenomenon enjoyed across all demographics and remains very popular. Poems are recited, almost always from memory, toasts proposed and songs sung. 'Tam O' Shanter' is one of Burns' masterworks, and its rollicking narrative delights all who attend.

Walter Scott may be the only author ever to have a main-line railway station named after one of his novels, and nearby the spire of the Scott Monument towers over Edinburgh's Princes Street. But his novels are now little read. Unlike Burns, his readership has shrivelled into academic study. Nevertheless, his influence was profound. To some extent, we all live in Scottland.

23 The Fire of the Dram

Between 1858 and 1865, French winemakers began to realize that they had made a catastrophic mistake. Hoping to rejuvenate the rootstock of their vines, they had imported grafts from California, but it turned out that they carried a plague of something close to locusts, insects known as *Phylloxera vastatrix*. The American grafts were immune to the attentions of these little bugs, but the French vines were not. Famous vineyards were devoured and made rotten, and by 1865 it was clear that wholesale replanting would be needed. Wine production crashed as cellars were emptied, and the distillers of Scotch whisky smiled and rubbed their hands.

The Victorian tipple of choice had been brandy and soda, but after the ravages of *Phylloxera*, stocks vanished overnight. Into the alcoholic breach stepped Scotch whisky, and the acceptable substitute of Scotch and soda quickly became popular. Its acceptance was also much enhanced by the continuing literary success of Walter Scott romances such as *The Lady of the Lake, Rob Roy* and *Waverley,* as well as Queen Victoria and Prince Albert's near-obsessive love of Scotland and all things Highland. It was said that a glass of whisky brought a comely blush to the royal cheeks. In 1848, they bought the Balmoral estate, demolished the original house and built a grand mansion in what was known as the Scottish baronial style. Inside it the furnishings included tartan carpets and curtains. Walter Scott, *Phylloxera* and Victoria had combined to put the dram on the map.

Whisky had been distilled in the Highlands for centuries. The word is from the Gaelic *uisge beatha*, meaning 'the water of life', known as 'acquavit' in other cultures. *Uisge* is pronounced 'ishgay', and that was rubbed smooth into whisky.

The role of Islington Council in the development of the branding of Scotch whisky is sometimes overlooked. For long-forgotten reasons, bureaucrats from the north London borough had summonses served on two local landlords for selling whisky 'not of the nature, quality and substance demanded'. Perhaps they were watering it. The cases went to court in 1906, and under the provisions of the Merchandise Marks Act, the judge upheld the complaints, and in so doing almost accidentally defined the nature of Scotch whisky.

There was uproar in Scotland, and a great deal at stake. The problem was that the judge had formulated a very narrow definition. The only drink that could call itself Scotch whisky, he ruled, was one that was made in a traditional pot still, usually in a Highland distillery. No other drink could put 'Scotch Whisky' on its label. That was what horrified distillers in Scotland.

A new still had been designed in 1832 that could function continuously to produce industrial quantities of grain spirit. The product was clear, like gin or vodka, but the blenders added small quantities of what we now call malt whisky to give it some colour and character. Blends were cheap and popular, but a court case that originated in Islington ruled that they could no longer be labelled as Scotch whisky. Lawsuits were launched.

Eventually, a royal commission was set up and evidence gathered. The landlords of twenty-three pubs in Scotland and thirty-nine in England were astonished at what happened next. Posing as ordinary members of the public, government officials walked into their pubs and ordered a dram of Scotch whisky, but instead of drinking it, they poured what they were served into a bottle and took it away for analysis.

'On reference to the analyses, it will be seen that there is a very wide variation between whiskies from different distilleries; and that there is a very wide variation between different whiskies from the same distilleries in different years.' So said the royal commission, stating the blindingly obvious, at least to whisky drinkers. They went on: 'We have received no evidence to show that the form of the still has any necessary relation to the wholesomeness of the spirit produced ... we are unable to recommend that the use of the word "whiskey" [sic] should be restricted to the spirit manufactured by the pot-still process.'

Apart from an 'e' straying into the word, this was good news for the whisky blenders. And what was not to like about having whisky described as 'wholesome'? Then the royal commission addressed itself to branding. 'Our general conclusion, therefore, on this part of our enquiry is that "whiskey" is a spirit obtained by distillation from a mass of cereal grains saccharified [turned into sugar] by a diastase [an enzyme] of malt; that "Scotch whiskey" is whiskey, as above defined, distilled in Scotland; and that "Irish whiskey" is whiskey, as above defined, distilled in Ireland.' Phew! The blenders breathed a sigh of relief, but it was only a temporary respite.

Ten years later, more problems beset the Scotch whisky industry as its largest export market threatened to disappear overnight. In 1919, the Volstead Act ushered in the Prohibition era in the USA. For fourteen chaotic years, organized crime mushroomed on the illegal import and sale of alcohol. The Scotch whisky distillers unblushingly supplied smugglers. The reputation of one of them for authentic Scotch was so unwavering that his name went into the language. The phrase 'the real McCoy' came from Captain McCoy, whose cargoes of whisky were neither adulterated nor of poor quality.

Both malts and blends produced in Scotland now enjoy worldwide popularity, and some brands, as they should be, are treated with something close to reverence. In his magisterial *Scotch Whisky: Its Past and Present*, David Daiches wrote a characteristically elegant conclusion: 'The proper drinking of Scotch whisky is more than an indulgence: it is a toast to civilization, a manifesto of man's determination to use the resources of nature to refresh mind and body and enjoy to the full the senses with which he has been endowed.'

24 Aberdeen Angus

Old Grannie was much loved, especially where she was born and lived her long life, in the northeast Lowlands of Scotland. Having given birth to an astonishing twenty-five children, all of whom survived, she was also thought to be a marvel, and no one admired Old Grannie more than Queen Victoria. It happened that two days before she died, a portrait photograph was taken. The Queen and Prince Albert, saddened at the news, requested a copy of the photograph for Balmoral Castle. It was to be shown as part of the royal collection – of cattle photographs.

Old Grannie was the mother of the world-famous Aberdeen Angus breed. Entered first in the herd book as the 'prima cow', she was the progenitor on the dam side. In the county of Angus, her owner, Hugh Watson, had begun to breed big black bullocks with no horns, known as polled cattle. He did this to stop his beasts from injuring each other, especially when bulls were covering their cows.

Entered at number one in the herd book on the sire side is Old Jock, Hugh Watson's favourite bull. He covered Old Grannie seven times, and their calves were entered in agricultural shows from Perth to Moray. They won often, and Watson's polled cattle became very popular with other breeders. Their size and lack of horns also made them attractive in another important, and revolutionary, way.

William McCombie of Tillyfour in Aberdeenshire saw the future of cattle production very clearly and was a gifted publicist and salesman. The railway was coming, and a station had opened in Aberdeen in 1854. In the past, cattle had been driven on foot to market, often over very long distances. That meant they were smaller and needed to be more hardy, and when they did arrive at the market trysts at Crieff and Falkirk, their long treks had taken a toll. They had lost condition, and when buyers from the south came, they paid less for Scotch cattle than they might have, because they had to then drive them on to the fertile grass parks of East Anglia to be fattened before being sold at Smithfield in London. William McCombie realized that the coming of the rail network changed everything. Cattle could be fattened at home in Aberdeenshire and be in London in a day. And the bigger they were, the more money he would make. The polled cattle also had a head start, so to speak, in that those with horns were more difficult to transport by rail since the risk of injury in the packed cars was high.

To breed larger beasts, McCombie crossed his own Aberdeenshire stock with the descendants of Old Grannie and Old Jock from Hugh Watson's farm in Angus. The breed was born, and a brand was created. It was to be called Aberdeen Angus, no hyphen needed.

But that in itself was not enough. Just as the distillers of Scotch whisky had done, McCombie enlisted the favour of the royal family. In 1867, he entered one of his prime Aberdeen Angus bullocks for the Birmingham and Smithfield shows, taking him south by train. When McCombie's bullock won both supreme championships, he somehow wangled an invitation to Windsor

Castle so that he could show the beast to Queen Victoria. No doubt sporting his rosettes, the glossy black bullock was paraded around the Middle Ward courtyard. Perhaps he behaved and did not leave a deposit on the royal doorstep. The Queen was impressed and sadly, the bullock's fate was sealed. At Christmas 1867, McCombie had him slaughtered and prime cuts of Aberdeen Angus beef were sent to the palace by train.

Eighteen months later, Victoria came to Tillyfour while she was at Balmoral, only 30 miles (50 kilometres) away, to look over McCombie's wstock. She seems genuinely to have been interested. With the stamp of royal approval, business boomed, and Aberdeen Angus beef was in constant demand in fashionable London restaurants, the monarch setting trends as usual. The brand was securely established. In a slightly awkward gesture of thanks and acknowledgement, McCombie bought an outstanding yearling heifer that he promptly named The Queen Mother. Perhaps a little over-familiar, but propitious. He mated his heifer with a grandson of Old Jock and the result was one of the most fertile and prolific bulls in cattle-breeding history. The bloodlines of Black Prince of Tillyfour (a suitably distant royal reference) can be found in almost every Aberdeen Angus bull, cow and bullock – anywhere.

In 1873, four bulls bred from Tillyfour stock were exported to the USA. They were an immediate success. Bred with Texas Longhorn cows (their progeny remained polled), they did well on the open range and were hardy enough to endure the winter

winds and snows. Between 1878 and 1883, more than 1,200 Aberdeen Angus bulls and cows were sent to the USA. They became known as Black Angus cattle. It is now the most popular breed in North America.

What Americans like about Angus beef is its marbling, the thin streaks of intramuscular fat that run through it. This improves flavor and tenderness. William McCombie would have been very impressed with the prices the descendants of The Black Prince now fetch. In 2019, one bull was sold for $1.5 million. There are now more than 305,000 registered head of Black Angus cattle in the USA alone. Most graze the plains of Montana, Nebraska and Texas. Old Grannie would have been proud.

25 Tweed

Walter Scott's fame brought temporary fortune to him and enduring prosperity to the Border country he loved so deeply. But it was not only his novels and poems that put the south of Scotland firmly on the map. It was Scott's unlikely role as a fashion icon that helped create an industry and a brand.

Scott often wore a particular garment, one that spoke of the windswept, romantic hills and valleys of the Borders, as did his friend James Hogg, a gifted poet, novelist and temporary shepherd. There are several engravings of both men that show them wearing heavy woollen cloaks, known as the Shepherd's Maud, Check or Plaid. Made from homespun, undyed wool, these were woven in the Borders. With black yarn for the weft and white for the warp, or the other way round, to make a rectilinear pattern, local looms turned out these plaids to keep shepherds not only warm in the winter hills, but also dry. The natural waterproofing of the lanolin in the wool was very welcome when the rain and snow fell.

By wearing the Lowland equivalent of Highland tartan, Scott and Hogg made the Shepherd's Maud famous, and very attractive to their readers. It was much more than cloth; it signified a way of life celebrated and romanticized in the writings of both men. Hogg's well-worn soubriquet was the Ettrick Shepherd. Those interested in fashion began to improvise. In the early

19th century, nothing was worn for trousers except plain colours known as drabs, greys and blacks, and always with a dark jacket. Tailors were asked to adapt the Shepherd's Plaids, and make trousers out of them. It was the beginning of a trend and a step towards the invention of a staple item of menswear.

There was a difficulty, but one that the weavers in the Borders quickly solved. The undyed white wool in the Shepherd's Check tended to have a good deal of grey in it, and this made the trousers look dirty, a little too rustic. That did not matter on a December day in the hills, but it looked bad in a city street. Dyestuffs fixed the problem, and soon brown and black, blue and black and green and black checks were being turned out.

Enter an entrepreneur. James Locke was an expatriate Scot who had a fashionable tailor's shop in London's Regent Street. With Scott and Hogg's unwitting help, he was instrumental in creating an industry and a world-famous brand.

Locke kept an occasional diary of his dandyish life, and often used the royal 'we': 'We had been long familiar with the "shepherd's maud", and, we believe, were the first to wear one in town. Well do we remember, about 1833, going down High Holborn on a Sunday morning with a whole host of admiring followers behind us. What lots of these were made in the next ten years for travelling purposes. The maud was an article that added much to the Scotch trade, and they were soon produced in all the clan tartans. We remember to have sold one for a bedcover to the present Pope, and Lady Franklin gave one to all the officers of the ships going to seek for the North-West Passage.'

In London, Locke and his friends took to wearing matching jackets and trousers cut from bolts of Shepherd's Check. Other fabrics began to be used, and gradually the mens' suit evolved. And it has never gone out of fashion. When the Prince of Wales, the future King Edward VII, went shooting in the Scottish Highlands on the estates of the Earl of Seafield, near Inverness, he was much taken by the specially made suits of Shepherd's Check worn by the gamekeepers. He had suits made like them; the 'Prince of Wales Check' is still in vogue.

The term 'Tweed' was a deliberate invention of James Locke. Here he is trying to meet the demands of the market in tailoring and overcome the conservatism of the Galashiels textile-mill owners: 'When gentlemen of the rod and gun began to enquire for that which would resemble the shooting ground, we had nothing of the kind, neither was there any in the market. We wrote to a Galashiels house for a "range", but they replied that they had never heard of such an article. By the following post we requested them just to imitate Buckholm Hill which overshadowed them, at this time in beautiful bloom. A boy was despatched to bring some heather. Now when a handful of this was squashed together it had different shades varying with the seasons. This proved to be the very thing we wanted, and led to the introduction of a variety of colourings before unknown. This was the origins of the heather mixtures.'

When samples of the cloth, essentially pattern books, arrived at Locke's Regent Street shop in 1847, an oft-repeated tale recounts that he misread the label of Tweel for Tweed. And so a brand was accidentally invented. Given that the recipient of the fabled parcel was an expatriate Scot, a successful tailor and a visitor to Gala who knew where Buckholm Hill stood, none of this makes any sense. Locke knew fine what tweel was, and also where the Tweed flowed. Tweed cloth was almost certainly his deliberate invention, a smart piece of marketing that clearly branded cloth made in the Tweed Valley and associated it with the most famous Tweedsider in recent history, Walter Scott.

26 **Peter Pan**

 David Barrie was The Boy Who Wouldn't Grow Up. In the winter of 1866, two days before his fourteenth birthday, the elder brother of J. M Barrie went skating. Accidentally colliding with another skater, he fell on the ice, fractured his skull and died. When news of the tragedy reached his mother, Margaret Barrie, she resolved to 'get between death and her boy'. Of course, she failed, and David Barrie's death overwhelmed the family. He had been his mother's favourite, and she became obsessed with the boy who could never grow up. James Barrie remembered how he tried to fill the emotional void by dressing up in his older brother's clothes. In a bestselling biography of his mother, he wrote that once, when he came into her room, she said, '"Is that you?" I thought it was the dead boy she was speaking to, and I said in a little, lonely voice, "No, it's no' him, it's just me".'

James Barrie was born in 1860 in the Angus town of Kirriemuir, one of ten siblings. His education was peripatetic but rich. Two of Barrie's elder siblings, Alexander and Mary Ann, had qualified as teachers, and at the age of eight, he followed them to Glasgow Academy, where they taught, and they looked

after their little brother. Later they went to Dumfries Academy. It was there that the story of The Boy Who Wouldn't Grow Up began to stir into life. Barrie befriended Hal and Stuart Gordon, whose home and wooded garden at Moat Brae House was close to the school. He remembered it well.

'When the shades of night began to fall, certain young mathematicians shed their triangles, crept up walls and down trees, and became pirates in a sort of Odyssey that was long afterwards to become the play of Peter Pan. For our escapades in a certain Dumfries garden, which is enchanted land to me, were certainly the genesis of that nefarious work. We lived in the tree-tops, on coconuts attached thereto, and that were in a bad condition; we were buccaneers and I kept the log-book

of our depredations, an eerie journal, without a triangle in it to mar the beauty of its page. That log-book I trust is no longer extant, though I should like one last look at it, to see if Captain Hook is in it.'

Barrie was determined to become a writer, and after three novels and some journalism he began to write plays. Having moved to London, he found success with the productions of *Quality Street* and *The Admirable Crichton* in 1901 and 1902.

Most days, Barrie took Porthos, his big Saint Bernard, for walks in Kensington Gardens, where he struck up a friendship with the Llewelyn Davies family, and in particular, their children, George, Jack and Baby Peter, as well as their nanny, Mary Hodgson. The boys enjoyed playing with his big, cuddly dog, and Barrie entertained them by waggling his ears and moving his eyebrows up and down, and by telling them stories. The cast of Peter Pan was slowly coming together.

At 5 foot 3 inches (1.6 metres), James Barrie was a small man, and perhaps that was one reason why children found him easy to talk to. When he met little Margaret Henley and her mother, another friendship grew, and a new Christian name was created. The child adored Barrie and called him 'My Friendy', but like some young ones, she had trouble pronouncing her Rs. Barrie's nickname came out Fwendy, and sometimes it was Fwendy Wendy. Aged only six, the little girl died, but her Fwendy made sure she was immortalized.

Some of the stories Barrie told the Llewelyn Davies children revolved around Baby Peter. The author insisted that babies had been birds before they were born and could fly. To prevent them escaping, parents had bars attached to nursery windows. Barrie's tale was about one baby who did escape and flew out through the nursery window, eventually reaching Neverland (second to the left and straight on till morning), never to grow up.

The ghosts of David Barrie and Margaret Henley, the garden at Moat Brae House and its pirates, Barrie's big dog and the Llewelyn Davies children all came together in 1904 on the opening night of *Peter Pan, The Boy Who Wouldn't Grow Up*.

The play was an instant, enormous and enduring success. The indelible, wholly original image of Peter Pan has entered our culture. Barrie's dramatic genius gave the boy a dark, anarchic side to his character. When the stature of Peter Pan was unveiled in Kensington Gardens in 1912, there was disappointment. The sculptor, Sir George Frampton, had used a conventionally good-looking child as a model, and Barrie was not impressed. 'It doesn't show the devil in Peter.'

Having enjoyed great success with other plays, such as *What Every Woman Knows* and *Dear Brutus*, James Barrie was knighted in 1913, later made a member of the Order of Merit and elected Rector of the University of St Andrews in 1919. In 1922, he stood up to give a memorable rectorial address on the theme of courage. But he himself appeared to lack what he was about to talk about. Having stood silent at the lectern for a few minutes, paralysed by nerves, Barrie only began to speak after students started to barrack him. Perhaps such anxiety was not untypical. In a photograph taken only a few weeks later, Barrie's unsmiling face looks haunted, hunted, with dark circles under his eyes, hollow cheeks and a faraway, unreadable, almost vacant look.

Peter Pan grew out of tragedy, out of the deaths of David Barrie and Margaret Henley, and even more bereavement was to follow. George Llewelyn Davies was killed in action in Flanders in 1915, his brother, Michael, drowned in 1921, perhaps committing suicide, and Peter had an unhappy life. In 1960 he threw himself under a train. Barrie had little consolation at home. He married Mary Ansell in 1891, but they had no children of their own. When he learned that his wife was having an affair in 1909, they eventually divorced. So much tragedy swirled around Peter Pan and his creator, it is no wonder that the eternal innocence of children seemed like a refuge.

MOUBRAY HOUSE

27 Ugly Scotland

 In the early 1930s, Esta Henry opened an antique shop on the ground floor of Moubray House, where Daniel Defoe had taken lodgings in 1706. After the medieval stalls that used to be erected on Edinburgh's High Street, she called it The Luckenbooth. The shop was a favoured haunt of royalty. Queen Mary, the widow of George V, used to rummage around in it, and in 1948 it was visited by Queen Elizabeth, later The Queen Mother, and Princess Margaret. While they were there, Esta (perhaps she introduced herself formally as Esther) took mother and daughter upstairs to where Defoe had watched in terror as the Edinburgh mob protested the union. Queen Elizabeth was charmed, and said that Moubray House was where one 'would like to live on the Royal Mile'. Perhaps she had little notion of Esta Henry's past associations.

Despite being Jewish, Henry had joined the Protestant Action Society in 1936. Founded by John Cormack in 1930, it was violently anti-Catholic and anti-Irish immigration, as well as being very conservative in its religious beliefs. In June 1935, a huge riot was incited by Cormack in, of all places, the well-set, leafy suburb of Morningside, a byword for propriety and seemliness. A Eucharistic Conference had been organized by the

Catholic Church in Scotland, the first since the Reformation, and around 10,000 worshippers were expected to attend an outdoor service. Not only was St Peter's Catholic Church in Morningside, so was St Benet's, the official residence of Archbishop Andrew MacDonald. In the days before the service, he sent a letter to *The Scotsman*:

'The office which I have the honour to hold has been the object of gross insult and of the vilest accusations. For some time it has hardly been possible for a priest to appear in the city without being subjected to unspeakable indignities. They have been not only the target for vile abuse and most filthy and obscene language, but they have repeatedly been spat upon and molested in public streets. In the factories and public works Catholic employees, and particularly defenceless girls, have suffered bitter persecution, as contemptible as it is cowardly, and strenuous efforts have been made to induce employers to dismiss Catholics on the ground of their religion alone.'

On the evening of 25 June, around 10,000 supporters of the Protestant Action Society, egged on by John Cormack, flooded the streets of Morningside. They attempted to break through a police cordon to disrupt the service, and when the terrified worshippers attempted to leave, their buses were stoned. At a famous crossroads known as Holy Corner (there are four churches there), unholy violence erupted when the rioters overturned a bus full of men, women and children. Mounted police charged them. Despite this extraordinary event, nine members of the Protestant Action Society, including Esta Henry, were elected to the Edinburgh Corporation to serve as councillors.

Such vicious sectarianism was not confined to Edinburgh. In 1920, Alexander Ratcliffe founded the Scottish Protestant League in Glasgow, and in 1933 they won twenty-three seats on the city's council. By the end of the 1930s, with the looming approach of war with Germany, most of these extremists had faded away. But not all of them. It should not be forgotten that John Cormack remained an Edinburgh councillor until 1963.

28 The Stop Line

On the night of 8 April 1940, Colonel Birger Eriksen stood on the ramparts of the Oscarsborg Fortress. Built on a small island, it commanded a narrow strait in the long Oslofjord, defending Norway's capital from a seaborne invasion. Through his binoculars, Eriksen looked south, peering into the darkness. He had received an alarming signal from a fortress at the mouth of the fjord. A flotilla of unidentified warships was sailing northwards, towards the Oscarsborg, and beyond it, to Oslo.

Norway was formally neutral in the Second World War, and Eriksen had no orders from his superiors to deal with what he suspected was a German invasion. He also had a much-weakened garrison, and was unable to fire its lethal weapon. A secret, land-based torpedo battery had been installed on the island, but the officer who knew how to operate it was on sick leave. Eriksen quickly wrote a note, and told a sailor to take his launch across the fjord to the little town of Drobak, go to the house of Andreas Anderssen and wake him. Norway had urgent need of him, even though he was seventy-eight years old and had retired from the army in 1927. Eriksen asked the old man to take his uniform out of the wardrobe, dust it and himself down and rejoin the army. Anderssen had overseen the installation of the torpedo battery.

Meanwhile, the German flotilla was approaching fast from the south. Eriksen ordered the whole garrison on the Oscarsborg to stand to, armed and ready to receive orders. Quite what they might achieve with small arms and conventional artillery, he was not sure, particularly since almost all of them were raw recruits. He desperately needed the torpedo battery to be operational; these warships would be heavily armed, and could fire at the fortresses shore guns at point-blank range when they entered the straits.

Out of the darkness, the colonel at last made out the launch crossing the fjord from Drobak. Once inside the semicircular walls of the fortress, Lieutenant Colonel Anderssen saluted and immediately asked the commander what his orders were. Within the hour, the old man had completed an inspection of the battery and had torpedoes brought forward and loaded into their tubes, armed and ready to fire.

Around 4 o'clock in the morning, lookouts on the southern-most promontory of the Oscarsborg saw the looming shape of a large battleship leading a flotilla of smaller craft. At least one of these was heavily armed, and the others were probably troop transports. Eriksen called down to the torpedo battery to alert Anderssen, and he made ready to fire. As the ships steamed into range, showing no lights or identification, the colonel alerted the old man; 'Either I will be decorated,' he shouted down the telephone, 'or I will be court-martialled. Fire!'

Unsuspected by the Germans, the torpedoes scored direct and devastating hits, as did the shore batteries. The leading battleship caught fire, suddenly blazing in the darkness, lighting a scene of carnage on the waters of the fjord. It began to sink, passing close to the walls of the Oscarsborg Fortress, and the Norwegian defenders were certain they could hear the men on the stricken ship singing '*Deutschland, Deutschland über alles.*'

This extraordinary incident was the first action of the Second World War in Western Europe. The sinking of the battleship delayed the invasion of Norway long enough to allow King Haakon and his government to get away from Oslo with the country's gold reserves and prolong resistance for another two months. As it was bound to, the German invasion succeeded, and while it expanded Hitler's empire and gave easier access to Sweden's iron ore, there was a far more important strategic purpose behind it. The Germans shamelessly violated Norwegian neutrality in order 'to give our navy and air force a wider start-line against Britain'.

Having overrun Poland, Denmark and Norway, Hitler's High Command launched their armies against the Netherlands, Belgium and France. Memories of the static trench warfare of the First World War were fresh, and not even the most optimistic Wehrmacht generals could have predicted the collapse of France in a matter of days and the disaster at Dunkirk. While many soldiers were rescued from the beaches, the British army lost most of its heavy equipment: more than 1,000 field guns, 850 anti-tank guns and 600 tanks, as well as a vast arsenal of smaller arms and ammunition. In June 1940, Britain was suddenly left almost defenceless.

Winston Churchill had taken over as Prime Minister from Neville Chamberlain on 10 May 1940. His Foreign Secretary, Lord Halifax, supported by Chamberlain, was pressing for a negotiated peace brokered by the Italians, who were still officially neutral. With the fall of France, only the Channel stood between Britain and invasion, and such troops as were available were concentrated in the south of England to meet it. That left Scotland dangerously vulnerable. A tiny garrison of between 5,000 and 10,000 soldiers had to guard a 500-mile (800-kilometre) coastline between Inverness and the Firth of Forth. Despite Churchill's famous exhortation, there were virtually no soldiers to fight on the beaches, since those that were stationed in the east of Scotland had to guard existing military installations. In the summer of 1940, the Germans could have walked in unopposed.

This mattered, and Churchill knew it. Even if the Germans launched only a diversionary attack across the North Sea, it could have radically changed the political as well as the military landscape. Ships could have tied up in the deep-water ports of Aberdeen, Peterhead or Fraserburgh and unloaded an entire panzer division. There were several aerodromes suitable for glider or paratrooper assault. The north of Scotland could have been overrun in a matter of days.

If that had happened, leaving a substantial part of the British mainland controlled by the Germans, Churchill would have had no option but to sue for peace.

But there were no soldiers, or arms, to spare. Instead, geography was enlisted. Where the Grampian Mountains almost reach the sea at Stonehaven, there was a potential bottleneck. Having landed in Moray, Banff or Aberdeenshire, German panzers and troops would have to pass through this narrow corridor between the mountains and the sea. And that was where, in the summer of 1940, it was decided to build a 'stop line' – as quickly as possible.

Now almost completely forgotten, hidden by tree planting, overgrown by weeds and moss, the stop line built on the banks of the Cowie Water was all that would have stood between the Germans and the cities of the south of Scotland and beyond if an invasion force had been launched across the North Sea. The Cowie runs eastwards from the Grampians and into the sea at

Stonehaven. It is often steep-sided and a formidable obstacle to tanks, lorries and half-tracks. Men from 217 Pioneer Company and the Royal Engineers identified possible crossing points and bridges, and worked fast. They fortified them with pillboxes, concrete anti-tank cubes and barriers made from railway rails. In the mountains, it might have been possible to flank the Cowie stop line, and so the pass from Braemar down to Glenshee was also guarded by obstacles.

The streets and buildings of the town of Stonehaven itself were to be used as a barrier if invasion came, a necessary sacrifice to slow down the Germans and keep Britain in the war. On the night of 7 September 1940, the townsfolk thought that moment had come. The code word 'Cromwell' was issued, a warning that invasion was imminent. Church bells rang out an alarm, and many stood out on the seafront, searching the horizon, looking for the outline of a fleet. But there was none.

After 1945, the Cowie stop line was allowed to sink back into the banks of the little river. The concrete cubes at the bridges and crossings were moved aside, but the rest was left to be overgrown by history. The line is a monument to near-panic, to a threat that was all too real, but never came.

29 The Scottish Nazi

 On 4 September 1940, a day after Britain had declared war on Germany, the Conservative MP for Peebles and Southern Midlothian was composing a parody. In the library of the House of Commons, Captain Archibald Henry Maule Ramsay, known as 'Jock', converted 'Land of Hope and Glory' into 'Land of Dope and Jewry'. The descendant of an aristocratic family, he had become increasingly anti-Semitic in the 1930s, and also attacked the Soviet Union, claiming that the Comintern was dominated by Jews. His wife, the Hon. Mrs Ismay Ramsay, went even further. In a speech to the unsuspecting members of the Arbroath Business Club (the Ramsays lived in a nearby castle), she claimed that the British national press was 'largely under Jewish control and that an international group of Jews ... were behind world revolution in every single country,' and that Adolf Hitler 'must ... have had his reasons for doing what he did.'

There were objections to such a flagrant parade of prejudice from the Edinburgh Jewish Congregation, and in the Borders, Ramsay's constituency association were not happy. Goodness knows what the bankers, solicitors and accountants of the Arbroath Business Club made of it all. But Ramsay's views, and his wife's, were tolerated.

For them, the Jews were everywhere. Encouraged in what he saw as his valiant efforts to free the Conservative Party from the indisputable fact that it 'relies ... on Jew money', Ramsay decided to form the Right Club. Its 'main objective', he wrote, 'was to oppose and expose the activities of organized Jewry.' There were 135 male and 100 female members, many of whom were pillars of the British establishment. At first, the Right Club was chaired by the Duke of Wellington, and meetings were attended by the Duke of Westminster, Lord Redesdale (the father of the Mitford sisters, of whom Unity met and admired Hitler), Lord Lymington and others.

A cypher clerk who worked at the American embassy, Tyler Kent, joined the club, and because he had diplomatic immunity, Ramsay entrusted the membership book to him for safe-keeping. Their relationship began to stray into something akin to treachery. Kent was stealing documents detailing the content of correspondence between Winston Churchill and Franklin Roosevelt, the US President. Ramsay realized that America's involvement in the war would probably turn it in the Allies' favour, and he planned to make these exchanges public and thereby compromise vital diplomatic efforts. What he did not know was that the Right Club had been infiltrated by MI5 agents. Churchill and his cabinet feared that Ramsay might use parliamentary privilege to publicize what Kent had given him, and so it was decided to arrest both the American and the MP.

On 23 May 1940, Captain Archibald Ramsay was arrested and immediately sent to Brixton Prison. There was no trial, and he spent more than four years behind bars. In 1952, Ramsay wrote *The Nameless War*, an autobiographical attempt to justify his views and actions during and before the war. It was full of crazy ideas: the reformer Jean Calvin was a secret Jew whose real name was Cohen, Oliver Cromwell was a Jewish agent, and the real purpose of the execution of Charles I was to allow the Jews to come back to Britain. All of this was written after the appalling details of the Holocaust had become clear.

30 The Battle Rant

Pipers were not mere musicians. Highland armies used the bagpipes in the same way that others used the bugle, to send messages and sound the charge or, less often, the retreat. But perhaps pipers' most important military role was to skirl out the battle rants. Before clansmen charged, they played their war music to remind men of who they were, where they had come from, and why they had come to fight.

Early on D-Day, the morning of 6 June 1944, Simon Fraser, 15th Lord Lovat, led the 1st Special Boat Service Brigade into battle, and as the landing craft ploughed through the spray and waves of Sword Beach, he remembered his clan's history. Beside Fraser was his personal piper, Bill Millin. This was something British High Command had expressly forbidden. Easy targets, pipers had been slaughtered as they exhorted men out of the trenches of World War One and over the top. The generals had decreed that pipers should only be deployed in the rear of advancing armies, but the Chief of Clan Fraser ignored them. 'That's the English War Office,' said Fraser when Private Millin cited the regulations, 'You and I are both Scottish and that doesn't apply.' The truth was that the Highlander loved the idea of the military traditions of the clans being at the very forefront of the Normandy Landings, the liberation of Europe and the destruction of Hitler's evil empire.

As the ramp of the landing craft began to creak, was slowly let down and his comrades waded ashore under withering fire from German defenders, Millin blew hard to inflate the bag of his pipes, adjusted the drones and started to play. The soldier next to him was shot in the face and killed instantly, his body dropping into the crimson sea. But above the deafening explosions and the rattle of machine guns, Millin did not hesitate, playing *Highland Laddie*, a Jacobite song that harked back to the last time that Frasers charged an enemy with their pipers – at the Battle of Culloden. Marching up and down the sandy shoreline as bullets whipped and ripped around him, Millin played *The Road to the Isles* and *All the Blue Bonnets Are Over the Border*. He was the only soldier in the Normandy landings who wore a kilt. It was the tartan of the Cameronians, worn by Millin's father in Flanders, during the First World War. He was also almost unarmed, his only weapon the ceremonial dagger, the *sgian dubh*, tucked in the top of one of his stockings. As his comrades struggled up the beach, many of them hit, some killed, the piper kept playing. His courage and his music seemed to give them strength of will and mind.

Even before they reached the French coast and the great invasion armada was sailing in darkness out of the Solent, Lord Lovat had his piper play over a loudspeaker so that other ships close by could hear his music. One of the many commandos in the British contingent, Roy Cadman, was an Englishman, but the pipes still had an effect on him and many other soldiers: 'As we pulled out with Bill Millin playing his bagpipes, all the boats started tooting their hoots and all the men on the decks were cheering. It reminded us of footballers playing

for England against Germany, coming out of the tunnel onto the pitch, where all the crowd all cheered as they came out. It was just like that ... I'd seen some very tough lads there, the tears were running down their face due to the emotion that was being stirred up.'

An easy and very obvious target, the drones of the pipes clear against the background of the sea, it was a miracle Millin got off Sword Beach unharmed. Later, captured German snipers claimed they did not shoot at him because they thought he was *dummkopf*, not right in the head. When Millin was interviewed after the war, he said:

'When I went onto the beach other people were furiously digging in. Other Commando had managed to get off the beach but my group ... had been pinned down. I was standing at the water's edge with Lovat when the Brigade Major came up and said the Paras had captured the bridge at Bénouville. Lovat turned to me and said "Now Piper, do you mind very much playing the *Road to the Isles*. You can march up and down a bit if you wish." I thought it was rather an odd thing when the beach was under fire ... the noise was terrific. Anyway, I struck up the bagpipes and marched up and down; the comments I received, some were complimentary, others were not so complimentary.

At the time it didn't cross my mind about being killed but on reflection ... I wondered why they didn't kill me coming ashore when many others were killed and wounded. I think I was lucky, but being a young man I didn't think I was the one going to be killed. Later prisoners said they didn't shoot me because they thought I was mad!'

Once his unit had managed to get off the beach and strike inland, Millin kept playing. One of his comrades, Tom Duncan, said: 'I shall never forget hearing the skirl of Bill Millin's pipes. It is hard to describe the impact it had. It gave us a great lift and increased our determination. As well as the pride we felt, it reminded us of home, and why we were fighting there for our lives and those of our loved ones.'

Unarmed, with men dying around him, Bill Millin's weapons were the pipes and the music was his ammunition.

31 Tom Johnston

 The night of 13 March 1941 was clear, and the moon glinted off the surface of the Clyde as the great river wound its way north to the firth and the sea beyond. Navigators in the nose of the first wave of German bombers could easily make out the sprawl of Glasgow, despite the blackout, the river that runs through it, and their target, the industrial town of Clydebank. The first wave dropped a huge tonnage of incendiary bombs to light the way for those that followed.

Twelve-year-old Isa MacKenzie was talking to her father, getting ready for bed with her twin brother, Donald. Their mother had gone out for the evening. The MacKenzies lived on the top floor of a tenement building near the Singer Sewing Machine factory, which had been converted to turning out munitions. At 9 o'clock, Isa and her father heard the wail of air raid sirens: 'My father got us dressed in our best coats and took us downstairs, into the hallway of a room-and-kitchen flat on the bottom floor. One lady stayed at the front entrance and, whenever she heard a bomb whistle, she would shout "Duck!" and we would all have to get down. When we heard the slap, slap, slap, slap we thought it was tiles falling from the roof, but it was the incendiary bombs. We were there for five hours then the lady shouted, you have to get out, the building's on fire. We tried the brick shelters but they were only half built, with walls but no roofs.'

Isa, her brother and father dodged bullets as they sought shelter, eventually finding refuge in a billiards club as bombing continued through the night. After the all-clear sounded, at 7 o'clock in the morning, they emerged to find their building had been reduced to rubble. When Isa's mother was reunited with them, discovering everything they owned had been destroyed, they quickly made the decision to flee Clydebank, which had been put under martial law. 'It was like being in a horror film, passing the Singer wood yard and the tanks and Bowling and the whole place was just flames. This was something we had never thought about. We had seen it in the news in the cinemas, Coventry and London, but we never gave it a thought that one day this would be us.'

A second air raid took place on the night of 14 March, only a day later. Clydebank was almost completely destroyed. Of its 12,000 flats and houses, only 8 were undamaged. Official casualty figures listed 528 dead and a further 617 seriously injured, but the real death toll was probably double that. As in many industrial towns and cities, housing and factories were very close to each other since most people walked to work. But in the event, there was far less damage done to the Luftwaffe's main strategic targets: John Brown's shipyard, Beardmore's Diesel Works, the Singer factory and a Royal Ordnance factory.

Aware that such devastating raids might affect morale as well as munitions production, and to avoid industrial unrest, Winston Churchill appointed a seasoned, much-respected Labour politician to be Secretary of State for Scotland and gave him wide-ranging, independent powers. Tom Johnston seized the opportunity, and from the smoke and rubble of Clydebank, he was determined that he would begin to build a better Scotland and a better Britain.

Fearing more air raids, especially on the heavy industry of the west of Scotland, Johnston set up the Emergency Hospital Service. At safe locations, well away from cities and factories, at Raigmore in Inverness, Peel in the Scottish Borders, Law in North Lanarkshire, Stracathro in Angus, Ballochmyle in Ayrshire and Bridge of Earn in Perthshire, hospitals were quickly built to cope with a flood of casualties. New annexes were added to existing hospitals and several of Scotland's grandest country-house hotels were commandeered as convalescence facilities.

When the expected bombs did not fall, and after Pearl Harbour brought America into the war, Johnston did not hesitate. Using his dictatorial powers as Secretary of State, he filled the empty hospitals with patients whose care and operations had been delayed because of the war, or because they could not afford them. By 1944, more than 33,000 Scots had been treated, and none had paid a penny. Through a mixture of opportunism, idealism and guile, Tom Johnston had shown how a national health service might work in practice.

The tide of history was running with him. The war cabinet knew that a citizen army would never again submit to the sort of wholesale slaughter seen on the Western Front between 1914 and 1918. Men had to know what they were fighting for, what life would be like after the war. It certainly could not be a return to the misery and unemployment of the 1920s and 1930s. There needed to be a great deal of thought given to what a post-war Britain might be like, and so William Beveridge, an economist who was Master of University College, Oxford, was asked to write a report. In it, he set out the principles of what came to be called the 'welfare state'. His proposals were welcomed, and Tom Johnston and Ernest Brown, the Minister of Health, drafted a White Paper based on it, describing how a National Health Service might work. The example of the Emergency Hospital Service was crucial in persuading parliament that it could be successful, realistic and adequate. On 9 February 1944, the White Paper was approved by the war cabinet, and Britain changed.

After hostilities in Europe had ended in May 1945, the first general election for ten years was held on 5 July. Because so many voters were still serving in the armed forces, the results were not declared until 26 July. They stunned everyone, except the British voters. World opinion could not understand how it was an inspirational war leader like Winston Churchill could be turned out of office when the victory he had promised was achieved. And it was no close-run thing. Labour won in a landslide, gaining 393 seats that gave them a majority of 145 in the House of Commons.

It was clear that servicemen and women had overwhelmingly voted Labour. There were three main reasons for such a swing. Many believed that Churchill had needlessly prolonged the war, demanding unconditional surrender, a policy that was thought to have cost many lives on both sides. It was also a widely held view that change was needed. Within only twenty years, the ruling classes had led Britain into two world wars, and now different leadership was needed. And crucially, the Conservatives did not fully support the Beveridge Report. They said they were behind its principles, but worried publicly how a new health service was to be paid for.

As Minister of Health in Clement Atlee's Labour government, Aneurin Bevan delivered the National Health Service. By the time it came into effect, in the summer of 1948, Tom Johnston had retired from parliamentary politics. But he knew it would work. He had made it work in Scotland.

32 Stone Broke

 In 1949, the post-war idealism that swirled around a different future for Scotland was characteristically couched in the language of the past. A new Covenant was drawn up for the nation, and two million Scots, 40 per cent of the population, signed it. The principal aim of the Scottish Covenant was the revival of a parliament in Edinburgh, the return of what its supporters called 'home rule'.

The Labour government ignored the petition, saying that only one of Scotland's 71 MPs, the Liberal member for Orkney and Shetland, Jo Grimond, supported it, and in any case the issues were much too complicated to be decided by a referendum. Frustration among the membership of the Scottish Covenant Association began to build.

As the nights grew longer and colder in November 1950, a conspiracy was forming in the mind of a student at Glasgow University. What the cause of the Covenant needed was some drama, a symbolic act that would attract headlines. Ian Hamilton decided to commit what England would see as a crime and what Scotland should see as justice. After 650 years, a historical wrong would be righted. Hamilton resolved to break into Westminster Abbey, remove the Stone of Destiny from under the Coronation Chair, and return it to Scotland, where it belonged.

For many centuries, kings of Scotland had been crowned at Scone as they sat on the Stone of Destiny. The last to have done so was John Balliol in 1292. After humiliating him at Stracathro, Edward I of England had the stone taken south and installed under what was known as Edward the Confessor's throne. Since then, most English and British monarchs have been crowned as they sat on the Stone of Destiny (though not quite on it – its chilly and rough texture might have been uncomfortable for a royal posterior during a long ceremony, and so carpenters fitted it under a wooden seat), including the present queen.

It was Scotland's stone, looted in the Wars of Independence, and Ian Hamilton planned to bring it back to its rightful home. His first problem was that he had no money. The Chairman of the Scottish Covenant Association and at that time the Lord Rector of the University of Glasgow was John MacCormick, and when Hamilton went to see him, the student left with £50, a nod and a wink. After visiting London and Westminster Abbey on a recce, the young student decided that the Stone should be taken in the dead of night, after 2 o'clock, when the nightwatchman had finished his rounds. But Hamilton could see that the Stone was large and heavy, and at least two people would be needed to carry it off. So he began to recruit fellow conspirators.

Amazingly, the plan remained a secret even after Hamilton had spoken to several likely individuals, all of whom refused to help. Glasgow University traditionally marks the end of the winter term with Daft Friday and a dance at night. Hamilton invited a young domestic science student to be his partner. Kay Matheson, a fluent Gaelic speaker and a fervent supporter of the Scottish Covenant from Wester Ross, agreed to help. She might not manage to lift the Stone, but she could drive a car.

In the days that followed, Hamilton managed to recruit two other male students.

A week later, Hamilton, Matheson and Gavin Vernon were driving south in an unheated 1938 Ford. It was late December, and they had to keep stopping because the windscreen kept icing up. In a Ford Anglia, another student, Alan Stuart, was also driving down to London. The plan was to get into Westminster Abbey when Christmas celebrations would be taking up everyone's attention, get the Stone, put it in one car and drive down to Dartmoor to hide it, while the other car would go in a different direction (Wales?) as a decoy if they were followed. Almost from the moment they reached London, everything began to unravel.

In the late afternoon of 23 December, Ian Hamilton entered the abbey as a visitor. He hung around until closing time before hiding himself under a cleaner's trolley and pulling his overcoat over his head. Much later, when the coast was clear, he would open the doors to let in his fellow conspirators. But Hamilton was almost immediately discovered by the night-watchman. Convincingly claiming that he had been inadvertently shut in, instead of being detained, he was ushered to the door. The nightwatchman wished him a Merry Christmas.

In a hurried conference in the Ford Anglia, the four students decided they would simply break in. Hamilton had brought a burglar's toolkit, including a long and heavy jemmy, and late on Christmas Eve, they prised open one of the side doors of the abbey. It was in complete darkness and no torchlight beams swept across the great nave – and there it was, under the seat of the Coronation Chair, the Stone of Destiny, Scotland's Stone.

Having cracked and splintered the ancient wooden housing, the three young men pulled out the Stone. It was very heavy,

much heavier than Hamilton had thought. They were forced immediately to let it down onto the floor. Where it broke. Into two pieces. The students were horrified.

Gathering their wits, whispering to each other in the echoic abbey, they changed their getaway plan. While Kay Matheson ran out of the side door to get the Ford Anglia, Ian Hamilton was able to pick up the smaller fragment, about a quarter of the whole, and he bundled it into the boot of her car.

Matheson quickly drove off. She had a friend who lived in the Midlands, and would stay there until the hue and cry died down after the discovery of the removal (it was never thought of by any of the students as a theft – it was Edward I who been a thief) of the Stone in the morning. Then she would drive north to Scotland. But when she stopped too quickly at a set of traffic lights in Knightsbridge, the boot of the Ford Anglia sprang open, and the fragment of the Stone of Destiny fell out onto the road. Having heard the crash, she backed up the car and somehow managed to lift the fragment back into the boot before driving off.

Meanwhile, Hamilton and his fellow students had managed to lift the much bigger piece onto his overcoat and, using it like a sledge, they were dragging it across the floor of the abbey towards the door. Once they reached it, Hamilton made off to bring the old Ford closer, but when he put his hand in his pocket for the car keys, they were not there. They must have been dropped and, not having a torch, he lit matches to search the ground for them, retracing his steps. Near the abbey door, he stood on something hard. He had found the car keys.

Having heaved the large fragment into the old Ford, the Glasgow students almost immediately got lost in the London suburbs. Instead of driving southwest towards Dartmoor, they were going southeast into Kent. Improvising once more, they found an empty field, and in the half-light of dawn on Christmas Day, they buried their bit of the Stone of Destiny, and then made their way back to Scotland.

The story was everywhere, all over the papers, and Christmas radio programmes were interrupted with the sensational news. Traffic on all cross-border roads was being stopped and searched by the police. The three men had no idea what had happened to Kay Matheson, but none of the coverage spoke of an arrest.

A week after they had buried the Stone, Hamilton and two other students, who had previously declined to be involved, drove down to Kent to retrieve it. But when they reached the field, it was occupied. A Romani group had camped right on top of the hiding place. After some discussion, they looked the other way while the object was dug up. At that point, the plan began to falter once more. In his superb account, Ian Hamilton admitted that they 'had no further ideas of what to do, or where to go.'

Kay Matheson had returned to Scotland with her fragment, and on April 11 1951, the Stone was left in the ruins of Arbroath Abbey at the high altar. Two years later, Queen Elizabeth was crowned, sitting not quite on it. The students were never prosecuted. Public opinion would probably have supported their escapade, and it was decided that it should be quietly forgotten. Finally, in 1996, before a general election, the Conservative government allowed the Stone of Destiny to be repatriated to Edinburgh Castle, where it is now on display.

In 2008, Ian Hamilton's excellent account, *The Stone of Destiny*, was republished with a poignant postscript by the author, at that time eighty-four years old:

'When on 25th March, 1707, James Ogilvie, Earl of Seafield, Chancellor of Scotland, signed the Act of Union, ending Scotland's ancient independence, and merging the two parliaments of Scotland and England into the United Kingdom Parliament, he threw down the quill with these words: "Now there's the end of an auld song". It may be, it just may be, that on Christmas Day, 1950, four young people wrote a new verse to that old song. Whatever we did, the song is still being sung.'

33 Scotch-Irish

At the inauguration of Richard Nixon as President of the United States on 20 January 1969, the preacher Billy Graham said a prayer for his country and its new leader. In the characteristic cadences of born-again Christianity, he spoke of America's forefathers and quoted George Washington. Had he wished to, Graham could have gone much further back in history. To his right stood Richard Nixon, and beside him, the outgoing president, Lyndon B. Johnson. When Graham finally intoned 'Amen', all three looked up at the same time, and a photographer caught the moment.

Square-jawed, steely, strong, beetle-browed, these were the faces of power. But they also shared history. Nixon, Johnson and Graham were all notorious names in the past, each one active in what were known as the Riding Times in the Scottish Borders in the 16th century. This was the era of the reivers, a clannish, criminal society where swords and spears spoke louder than the law. Weak Stuart kings and their regents could not control the widespread raiding and reiving of cattle, sheep and anything else that could be carried off on moonlit nights when these horse-riding thieves were abroad.

Johnsons, Nixons and Grahams were all feared, riding at the heart of a century of lawlessness. Blackmail originally meant 'black rent', and it began as a protection racket run by the reiving families. In return for payment, they agreed to not only leave a farmer's cattle alone, but also make sure that other reivers did not steal them. Blackmail and other nefarious ploys might have been a handy historical memory for Johnson, and especially Richard Nixon. Neither hesitated to use what might be termed heavy persuasion during their time in the White House.

Ironically, it is probably the case that Billy Graham's ancestors were the most consistently flagrant miscreants. When James VI became the I of Great Britain and Ireland, the border disappeared, and he set about pacifying what he called the Middle Shires. It had been useful for bands of reivers to be able to cross quickly from one jurisdiction to another to escape the law.

And so after Robert Carey's ride and James' accession there followed what became known as 'Ill Week', an outbreak of concentrated, almost frenzied, raiding, a last tearaway gallop before the inevitable crackdown began. As the bishop of Carlisle watched from the safety of the ramparts of the castle, Hutcheon Graham led a company of reivers through the meadows by the River Eden. Not troubling to conceal themselves, they were riding south to steal Cumbrian cattle. It was said that when Hutcheon Graham passed close to the castle walls, he looked up at the bishop and made a very rude gesture.

Richard Nixon and Lyndon Johnson were by no means the only American presidents to have links to Scotland. When James VI and I began to deal with the problem of the Border

reivers, one of his tactics was simply to expel them, and whole families were deported to Ireland in a process known as the Plantation of Ulster. Some kept on moving, and in America became known as 'Scotch-Irish'. Not all by any means were reivers, but they do appear to have had a talent for the rough and tumble of politics. No fewer than fourteen US presidents claimed descent from these immigrants. In fact, from 1829 to 1921, the White House was occupied for only twenty-five years by men who were *not* of Scotch-Irish descent.

Andrew Jackson, founder of the Democratic Party, was the first. He was said to be 'as tough as old hickory', and Old Hickory became his nickname. He was followed by James K. Polk, James Buchanan, Andrew Johnston, the great Civil War general, Ulysses S. Grant, Chester A. Arthur, Grover Cleveland, who served two non-consecutive terms, Benjamin Harrison, William McKinley, Theodore Roosevelt, Woodrow Wilson, Lyndon B. Johnson, Richard Nixon and Jimmy Carter, the last to claim a Scotch-Irish lineage – though Bill Clinton was born William Jefferson Blythe, and has family links with the Scottish Borders through his father's ancestry.

34 The Scottish Cringe

 At 6.20 p.m. on Wednesday 7 May 1958, a shaky caption on a black and white TV screen announced 'BBC Television in Scotland Presents *The White Heather Club*.' A uniformed commissionaire opened a glass door to admit the cameraman and the audience to what looked like the foyer of a modern office block, and then saluted. After a few moments, the viewers were welcomed by Andy Stewart. It was the launch of a cultural phenomenon. By 1961, *The White Heather Club* was broadcast all over Britain, and in an age when only between 60 and 70 per cent of households had TV sets the audiences were huge, regularly ten million and more.

The format was a weekly ceilidh, an informal party held in Highland homes where people did turns, their party pieces, at a time when they had to entertain themselves. In the TV version, the viewers first heard a specially composed accordion piece called 'The Six-Twenty Two-Step' from Jimmy Shand and his band. Then the party's host, Andy Stewart, would sing:

> *Come in, come in, it's nice to see you*
> *How's yersel', you're looking grand.*

In what always seemed a very cramped studio, Highland dances that might have been reels or strathspeys were heavily featured. Doing well not to bump into the furniture, the Dixie Ingram Dancers were in almost every show until *The White Heather Club* came off air in 1968. Each episode ended with the cast singing, *Haste ye back, I love you dearly. Call again, you're welcome here.*

It was a strange, mostly nauseating, version of Scottish culture, a random, cringe-making mash-up of bits and pieces from the Kailyard (a Lowland tradition of popular songs, usually about the countryside), what the producer imagined a ceilidh to be, and the Victorian obsession with tartan and the Highlands. The show was distressingly popular. What the English, the Welsh and the Irish made of it can only be imagined.

The viewing figures are a cultural riddle. There is no doubt that the presenter, Andy Stewart, was a gifted performer. A mimic as well as singer and composer, he carried a creaking, old-fashioned format virtually single-handed. Nevertheless, on the edge of his pawky humour and cheeky-chappie smile, there was more than a hint that he knew exactly what he was doing and how it worked. Swathed in tartan, performing only traditional music, *The White Heather Club* was undoubtedly a harking back to a past that never existed, a musical and televisual Brigadoon that appeared once a week for a decade. That may have been the core of its appeal, its distance from the smoky factories and the bustle of the cities of the central belt, where most Scots lived. This weekly presentation of a Scottish Neverland was also par-ticularly attractive to exiled Scots living in England. At the same time as The Beatles, The Rolling Stones, Bob Dylan and others were remaking popular music and inventing a youth culture, *The White Heather Club* was a comfortable, nostalgic wallow,

couched in what Andy Stewart called 'the swirl of the kilt and the skirl of the pipes.'

It was not only in England that the show and its charismatic presenter were popular. Following in the footsteps of Harry Lauder, another citizen of Brigadoon, Andy Stewart wrote popular songs such as *The Scottish Soldier* and *Donald, Where's Yer Troosers?* that were listened to worldwide. He toured the USA, Canada, Australia and New Zealand, packing theatres with those nostalgic for the mist-strewn hills of home. Sadly, Stewart was dogged by ill health, his recurring heart problems not helped by a punishing schedule of foreign engagements and long runs in Scottish theatres. He died in 1993, a day after appearing at the Usher Hall in Edinburgh to support a children's hospice charity, only fifty-nine years old.

The *White Heather Club* version of Scotland remains popular, but markedly less so with the passage of time. In many ways, the kilts, the tartan sashes and the pawky humour were part of a Scotland defined by England. Most of the elements of the show, including the format of the ceilidh, originated in the Highlands and in Gaelic. And what could be more different, more un-English? Walter Scott has a great deal to answer for.

Scotland is at its best when its horizons extend far beyond the Cheviots, to the rest of the world, as they did during the Enlightenment. When Scots retreat into the cloying, parodic world of tartanry, they are patronized, put in a box marked marginal, forever backward-looking – to a past that never existed.

35 Margot's Man
and Murray's Maw

If Scotland beat England every year, at any sport, rugby, football, bowls or table tennis, most Scots would be happy and believe that they belonged to a great sporting nation. As usual, this myopic view hides a much better story, one of real sporting achievement, often against the odds and featuring a series of remarkable, single-minded individuals.

Despite the climate, the lack of facilities and the restricted pool of talent that is five million Scots, the nation has produced great, world-class sportsmen and women. Jim Clark and Jackie Stewart were motor-racing world champions, Katherine Grainger, multiple rowing medallist, is the most successful female Olympic athlete ever, and Chris Hoy, the cyclist, is Britain's greatest Olympian, with no fewer than six gold medals. They and others would probably have flourished anywhere, such was their talent. It was, in truth, only the accident of birth that allowed Scots to bask in their reflected glory. But there are two world-class sportsmen who are different, quintessentially Scottish, whose upbringing and cultural attitudes fuelled their performances and made them steely competitors against the odds.

The 1980 Olympic Games were due to be held in Moscow, but six months before the flame was lit, the Soviet Union invaded

Afghanistan. In protest, many countries, including the USA, decided to boycott the games. Under Margaret Thatcher, the British government devolved any decision to the British Olympic Association, who in turn left it to the individual athletes to come to a personal view about their own involvement. Nevertheless, the government attempted to influence them.

When the Scottish sprinter Allan Wells opened his post one morning, he found a photograph of a dead Afghan girl with a doll lying a few inches from her outstretched arm. That convinced him. 'I just thought it was deplorable for the British government to be sending pictures like that. I think that was the breaking point for me and I decided that if that was the attitude then I was definitely going to go.'

At the age of twenty-four, Wells had been a failed long jumper, beginning to despair of his athletics career. In order to increase the speed of his run-up, and therefore the length of his jump, he began to train with Wilson Young. The relationship was emblematic of a historically uneasy link. Young had been a successful professional sprinter, winning the premier race of the year at Edinburgh's Powderhall Stadium in 1970. He trained alongside George McNeill, the holder of British records and a former professional footballer. The 'peds', as the professional runners were known, competed for cash prizes on the circuit of Highland and Border games. Races were handicapped, and gambling an integral part of the sport.

Allan Wells knew that these men took what they did very seriously, and he wanted to learn from Wilson Young. Within a very short time, the long jumper had become a sprinter, specializing in the 100- and 200-metre races. Wells began to win, but working with Young became more and more difficult. Adjectives like 'prickly' and 'self-willed' were attached, but Wells did not

compromise. 'I'm not out to make friends,' he said. He was out to win, and win his way.

Although Wilson Young moved on, he had passed on professional methods. Wells' wife, Margot, took over, giving up her own successful athletics career to coach her husband in a converted garage in Edinburgh, doing gym-style training. Particularly important was their work with the speedball, a boxing technique that sharpened reactions and strengthened the arms. In 1978, Allan Wells set a new British record for the 100-metre sprint, and was hailed as the best since Harold Abrahams won Olympic gold in Paris in 1924. He began to focus on Moscow.

Having won the first of his heats in the 100 metres, Wells faced a real test in the next round. With more than a whiff of gamesmanship, the Russians had put all of the best sprinters in one heat, except for their own. They were given a much easier passage to the final. But the Scotsman came through.

Margot Wells remembered that the coaches of the British team were worried about her husband the day before the Olympic final. He was far too confident of victory. What they failed to understand was that his attitude was entirely sensible. Relaxed sprinters sprint better, and faster. Wells knew that aggression and tension would slow him down.

But he was not happy about the draw. His closest challenger was the Cuban, Silvio Leonard, and he had been placed in lane one, while Wells had been allocated lane eight. It would be very difficult to race against someone he could not see for at least half the race. The Scot had the second-string Cuban in the next lane, and he focused on outrunning him, but in the final ten metres he seemed unable to overtake Leonard. But Wells dipped for the tape and managed to breast it fractionally before his rival, winning by centimetres. Even though the Russian officials took ten minutes to decide the result, Wells looked at the replay, knew he had won, and went on the victory lap around the stadium he had promised himself.

On the podium, there was no British national anthem and no Union Jack flew for the Scotsman. Both had been banned by the Thatcher government, the people who had sent Allan Wells the photo of the little dead girl. It did not matter. His focused, gritty determination had won him the gold medal. Showing great awareness of history as well as emotional intelligence, Wells dedicated his medal to Eric Liddell, another single-minded Scot. At the 1924 Olympics, Liddell was strongly fancied to win both the 100 and 200 metres, but when the heats for the former were scheduled on a Sunday, the committed Christian would not break the Sabbath and he pulled out. But he won the 200 metres.

Thirty-two years after the Moscow Olympics, another prickly, self-willed, determined Scottish athlete took the world stage and emulated Allan Wells' achievement. In 2012, Andy Murray won not only the US Open tennis championships but also an Olympic gold medal in London.

Murray has had eleven coaches in his career, and a reputation for being forthright in his views. When a BBC interviewer suggested that Murray was the first person to win more than one Olympic gold medal for tennis (he won again at the 2016 Games), he replied 'I think Venus and Serena [Williams] have won about four each.' And Murray's achievements have had a particularly anguished Scottish character. When he won his first Wimbledon title in 2013, he almost forgot to hug his mum. *The Herald* reported: 'A steward pointed out that Judy Murray was sitting in the row behind the players' box. He jumped into her arms with the realization that this was a journey shared and the fellow travellers may have been numerous, but he only has one Maw.'

After injury, great deal of pain and operations on his hips, Andy Murray is now nearing the end of a remarkable career. Here is part of a recent appraisal of his achievements from *The Guardian*:

Three things make him a man who really shifted the dial. The first is the way he changed how he himself was seen. When he first came to notice, Mr Murray was a gifted but introverted player who found it hard to win over the public. His outsider's awkwardness was often contrasted with the establishment entitlement of his predecessor as British number one, Tim Henman. Mr Murray was Scottish and had not risen through the system, training in France. 'Tory Tim', as some commentators dubbed him, was blazered and southern – and rose through the very traditional Lawn Tennis Association.

Mr Murray didn't try to reinvent himself. Instead he became a champion by doing it his own way. He made himself stronger and fitter, and honed his backhand into a lethal weapon. He began winning, which was a welcome change for a victory-starved British tennis public whose annual hapless shout – once dubbed the three most depressing words in the English language – was 'Come on, Tim'. He took over because he was better and more ruthless, but without compromising his less privileged background, his Scottishness or his determination to success on his own terms.

36 Reconvened

When Sheena Wellington's crystal voice rang out with 'A Man's a Man For A' That', Robert Burns' great anthem, on 1 July 1999, all Scotland rejoiced. It was the beginning of a new song and not, as the Earl of Seafield had said in 1707 when he signed the Act of Union, the end of an old one. When Winnie Ewing MSP presided over the opening session, her words were simple and unforgettable: 'The Scottish Parliament, adjourned on the 25th day of March in the year 1707, is hereby reconvened.'

But history had not come full circle. The journey to the new parliament was tortuous and fascinating. It began, and almost ended, with Winnie Ewing. In 1967 she won a spectacular by-election at Hamilton, near Glasgow, claiming the seat from Labour. A charismatic and energetic candidate, her first words after the result had been declared were 'Stop the world. Scotland wants to get on.'

It was a brief flicker, a stuttering start to the rise of the Scottish National Party. Ewing lost Hamilton in the 1970 general election, but with victory in the Western Isles for Donald Stewart, the party retained a presence at Westminster even though their share of the vote was 11 per cent. Under the Conservative government of Edward Heath, pressure for devolution, as home rule came to be called, stalled. There was another spectacular by-election victory in 1973, when Margo Macdonald won the Labour seat of Glasgow Govan, but she held it only for a year.

Heath's troubled administration fell as miscalculations were made. Having disputed with the National Union of Mineworkers and been forced to adopt a three-day working week because of energy shortages, the Conservatives called a snap general election in February 1974. They framed the issues around the general principle of 'Who Governs Britain?' The answer was 'Not You', and under Harold Wilson, Labour formed a minority government.

In Scotland, new dynamics were at work, with the discovery of off-shore oilfields in the North Sea that were served onshore in Orkney, Shetland and Aberdeen. With the potent slogan of 'It's Scotland's Oil', the SNP won seven seats. This was different

from catching fire only at by-elections, and when Wilson called a second election in October 1974, they picked up eleven seats.

There began a cycle of three referenda that would turn history in surprising directions. Responding to the success of the SNP, Labour under James Callaghan produced a White Paper that advocated not a parliament but a Scottish Assembly in Edinburgh with limited powers. This represented significant constitutional change and a referendum was proposed. But the Labour Party was split. A spoiler amendment was introduced by George Cunningham, a Scot who sat for a London constituency. He insisted that the first-past-the-post system used for Westminster be replaced. Those who voted for a Scottish Assembly would have to amount to more than 40 per cent of the electorate. This stipulation essentially settled the issue before a single vote was

cast, and even though those in favour, 32 per cent, turned out to be in the majority over the 30.8 per cent who rejected devolution, the bill fell.

The first devolution referendum was also overtaken by events. After the fabled 'winter of discontent', when public-service strikes disfigured towns and cities as rubbish was uncollected and the deceased left unburied, Callaghan was forced to call an election in 1979. It was precipitated by a motion of no confidence from the eleven SNP MPs, unhappy at the outcome of the referendum, and it prompted a famous quote from the Prime Minister. It was, he said, 'the first time in recorded history that turkeys had been known to vote for an early Christmas.' Margaret Thatcher won a majority for the Conservatives, and the SNP lost nine seats. But it was the beginning of an inexorable cycle that led eventually to a second referendum, and then to a third.

A key statistic that measures the rise of Scottish nationalism was not only the size of the SNP vote, but also what happened to the Labour Party in Scotland in the decades following Thatcher's victory in 1979. In that election the Labour vote in Scotland increased by 10 per cent and the party gained two seats in Scotland, whereas in England, their vote declined by 10 per cent and fifty seats were lost. In 1983, after the Falklands War, Margaret Thatcher won a landslide in England, but in Scotland the Conservatives lost a seat. An electoral gap was beginning to open, one that would widen into a chasm.

With many Scots, Margaret Thatcher's policies and personal style grated. After the failure of the miners' strike, the steelworks closures and much else, the speed of the rundown of heavy and manufacturing industries was dizzying. Government intervention was not encouraged, and unemployment grew as the industrial landscape quickly became a wasteland of deserted factories and broken windows. The Prime Minister was very unpopular, and an emblematic incident took place in the spring of 1988. At the General Assembly of the Church of Scotland held at the Assembly Hall on the Mound in Edinburgh, the nearest thing there was to a national parliament, Margaret Thatcher made a speech. It was remarkable, imperious, inappropriate; it became known as the Sermon on the Mound. As ministers and elders sat in silence, Thatcher attempted a theological justification for her policies: 'If a man will not work, he shall not eat, said St Paul,' and much more in that vein. She rebuked the Kirk for becoming involved in politics, and put it in what she thought should be its place: 'We parliamentarians can legislate for the rule of law. You, the Church, can teach the life of faith.'

In 1988, the Moderator of the General Assembly was the Rev. Professor James A. Whyte of St Andrews University. When he came down from the pulpit to greet Mrs Thatcher after her speech, he had with him two Kirk pamphlets on poverty and housing, which he hoped she would find interesting. But his most eloquent and elegant rejoinder to her remarks was his comment: 'Prime Minister, I do not think that you have ever been in the presence of so many people who pray for you regularly.'

Once again, a keen awareness of Scotland's history surfaced in political action. In 1689, the Scottish Parliament had passed the Claim of Right Act, voting to remove the Catholic James VII from the throne of Scotland and to offer it instead to William of Orange and his wife, Mary. It essentially asserted Scotland's right to act independently of England (and the act was used again in 2019 to rule Boris Johnson's prorogation of parliament as unlawful) in constitutional matters. In 1989, exactly 300 years later, a new Claim of Right was drafted, and this time its aim was to bring into being a Scottish Parliament.

On 15 November 1996, a farcical, almost pantomimic series of events took place. On a dreich, damp morning, in the back of an army Landrover followed by a white van that looked distinctly out of place, the Stone of Destiny made its way at a funeral pace across the Tweed Bridge at Coldstream and back into Scotland. The Conservatives would be forced to call a general election in 1997, their poll numbers were not encouraging, particularly in Scotland, and it was thought a worthwhile gesture to follow in Ian Hamilton's footsteps. The weather had brightened by the time the Stone reached Edinburgh Castle. It was accompanied by Prince Andrew and escorted by the Royal Company of Archers, old men in green uniforms carrying wooden bows and with long pheasant tail feathers stuck in their hats. Dressed in a kilt and surrounded by more colourful outfits (why do spectacles always look out of place on Heralds and others in elaborate, faux-medieval costumes?), Michael Forsyth, the Secretary of State for Scotland, read out a speech promising to take the Stone back to Westminster Abbey whenever it was needed for a coronation and then, like someone with a lottery cheque, he showed off a document with a pendant seal.

In the general election that followed, Forsyth lost his seat, as did all the other Conservative candidates in Scotland. The incoming Labour government immediately enabled a referendum on whether or not there should be a Scottish parliament. On 11 September 1997, almost 75 per cent of those who voted agreed that there should, and in 1999 the first elections were held. It felt to many that the end of a long road had been reached, but that turned out to be a false impression.

The Scotland Act of 1998 opened with a ringing phrase: 'There will be a Scottish Parliament,' and it set out its legislative competence, how many members it should have and how they should be elected. The last point became enormously important. Instead of only the first-past-the-post system, proportional representation was also to be used, to make sure more parties were represented. As the Liberals had done for decades, losing parties in constituencies could pile up large numbers of votes nationally but have very little representation in parliament. In essence, the electorate would have two different sorts of votes.

There were to be 129 MSPs, with 73 elected as constituency members using the first-past-the-post system, and 56 MSPs elected for so-called list seats in eight regions. Parties were to create ranked lists of candidates, and the D'Hondt method (designed by a Belgian mathematician in 1878 and used in forty countries today) would be used to calculate how many seats they should be allocated. The number of second votes cast would be divided by the number of constituency seats won by each party in the electoral region. So if SNP, Labour, Liberals or Conservatives did well in the constituencies, they would do less well on the lists. And parties that won no constituencies could be allocated seats. All of these things happened.

In the 1999 election, Labour won fifty-six seats, the SNP thirty-five, Conservatives eighteen (they won no constituencies but had a substantial national vote) and the Liberals seventeen, but for the first time the Green Party gained a parliamentary seat, as did the Scottish Socialist Party. In a parliament that was supposed to meet the home rule aspirations of the SNP and thereby make their existence redundant, they found a place, winning seven constituency seats and twenty-eight on the list allocation, polling 28 per cent of the vote.

The first sessions of the parliament sat in an adapted Assembly Hall in Edinburgh, the place where Margaret Thatcher had delivered the Sermon on the Mound. Costs for building the new parliament at the foot of the Royal Mile, opposite Holyrood Palace were estimated at around £40 million, but they soon ballooned. Designed by the Catalan architect Enric Miralles, it has some splendid interiors and the chamber is magnificent, but eventually the building cost a staggering and shaming £414 million. If the MSPs could not control the cost of their own building, could they run the country?

When the first session of the new parliament met in the Assembly Hall on 12 May 1999, the distinguished journalist, Ian Bell, was in the press gallery, writing for *The Scotsman*: 'Dr Winifred Ewing, sixty-nine, mother of the house, had already reminded us of what was being done. In the capital's grey Assembly Hall, just after 9.30am, to a half-empty chamber, she uttered the simple, astonishing truth: "The Scottish Parliament, adjourned on the 25th day of March, 1707, is hereby reconvened". History is memory. This moment was memory reclaimed, a right restated, a truth reaffirmed. The nation of Scotland, with all its thrawn suspicions, numberless confusions, apathy, clumsy rivalries and disparate hopes, had remembered.'

In 2007, the SNP won the Scottish election. By the slimmest of margins, one seat, they were the largest party, and historical ironies immediately abounded. They were able to govern because of an informal pact with the party of Margaret Thatcher, the Conservatives, and also two Green MSPs. On 30 November that year, Alex Salmond's government proposed a White Paper to bring forward a referendum on Scottish independence, but it found no support among the other parties and was dropped.

In 2010, the British general election saw no overall winner, and eventually the Conservative Leader, David Cameron, formed a coalition with the Liberal Democrats. In Scotland, perhaps as a result of the popularity of the outgoing Prime Minister,

Gordon Brown, there was a swing to Labour and a gain of two seats. Once again the electoral gap widened.

But in the 2011 Scottish election, Labour suffered badly, losing sixteen seats, and because of the UK coalition with the Conservatives, the Liberal Democrats were routed, but the SNP gained an overall majority. It was an astonishing result, the first time the largest party had not needed to form a coalition. They could govern on their own.

Now the SNP believed they had a mandate to bring forward legislation to allow a referendum on independence. Once again, politics in England had profoundly shaped what happened in Scotland. As in the era of Margaret Thatcher, the Cameron government was very unpopular north of the border, and acted as a helpful recruiting sergeant for the SNP. The collapse of Labour and the migration of its voters encouraged the nationalists to develop into a social democratic party. And after four years in government in Edinburgh, they were also seen as competent, credible, no longer a party with only one issue.

The Edinburgh Agreement of 2012 set the terms of a referendum and soon a date was fixed – by Alex Salmond, the First Minister. It was to be held on 18 September 2014, in the wake of the Commonwealth Games held in Glasgow, the Ryder Cup at Gleneagles and the 700th anniversary of the victory at Bannockburn. It was Scotland's year. Crucially, the SNP were also very influential in the framing of the question on the ballot paper. It was to be simply 'Should Scotland be an independent country?' To tick the 'Yes' box was seen as a positive, and the 'No' box was a negative. This greatly influenced the tone of the campaigns.

Better Together was an uneasy coalition of Labour, Conservatives and Liberal Democrats and it campaigned for a 'No' vote, but its messages were attacked as negative and its warnings as 'Project Fear'. As polling day approached, the opinion polls narrowed; some were very much within the margin of error, and two showed a slim majority for a 'Yes' vote. Former Prime Minister Gordon Brown had become independently involved, and to counter accusations of negativity, he and others compiled the 'Vow', a promise of more powers for the Scottish Parliament, an undertaking signed by David Cameron, Ed Miliband, the Labour Leader and Nick Clegg, the Leader of the Liberal Democrats. Most influential was a passionate speech made by Gordon Brown at midday on the day before the referendum. Soundbites ran on news bulletins but, even more important, it was uploaded on YouTube and watched by thousands of voters.

The turnout was unprecedented. On 18 September 2014, 84.5 per cent of the electorate voted and by a clear majority of 55 per cent to 45 per cent, Scotland decided to remain in the United Kingdom. Of all the local authorities, only Glasgow, Dundee, West Dunbartonshire and North Lanarkshire voted to leave.

But that did not settle the matter. The morning after the poll, David Cameron stood on the steps of 10 Downing Street and immediately handed the political initiative back to the SNP. He promised to enact legislation that would exclude Scottish MPs from voting on purely English legislation at Westminster. Danny Alexander, a Liberal Democrat minister in his coalition government was furious: 'Talk about trying to snatch defeat from the jaws of victory. What it did was just give the nationalists a whole grievance agenda from a minute after the result was declared. It was just dreadful.'

In the 2015 British general election, the bloc of the 'Yes' vote, 45 per cent, voted for SNP candidates and virtually wiped out all other parties in Scotland. Fifty-six out of fifty-nine

Scottish MPs were from the SNP, and Labour, Conservative and Liberal Democrats were left with one seat apiece. The effect of Labour's massive losses in Scotland was to hand Cameron's Conservatives a majority in the election, and it appeared that the announcement on the steps of Downing Street in 2014 had been a cold calculation.

Since then, two general elections have seen Conservatives continue in government, with Boris Johnson's victory of 2019 giving them a commanding majority of eighty seats. Under Nicola Sturgeon, the SNP have also remained in government, and once again momentum is building for another referendum on Scottish independence.

The gap has become a chasm, perhaps one that is unbridgeable. The United Kingdom faces an uncertain future.

Epilogue

At school, I much enjoyed history, and geography. Too young
to rationalize the link, I intuited that they fitted together like
the pieces of an unmade jigsaw to make a more or less complete
picture. History didn't just happen anywhere, in empty rooms
or deserted car parks; hunters hunted in the shadows of real
forests, monks prayed in holy places and Robert Bruce won at
Bannockburn because he understood geography and how to turn
it into a killing ground. And yet for most of my time at school
and all of my university career, it was impossible to study both
in tandem. The curriculum didn't allow it.

I never understood why such an obvious connection was
denied. First geology and then geography have profoundly
informed Scotland's history, since the retreat of the ice
12,000 years ago. And just as the primeval collision of the four
terranes made our geography unique, so it in turn made our
history different, and not just different from other nations but
also diverse in itself. There were and are many Scotlands. Not
only for amused outsiders, the synthetic tartanry promoted by
Walter Scott and others has blinded many Scots to the riches
hidden behind the clichés. Even within Highland, Gaelic-speaking Scotland, there was real difference between the Norse clans
of the Atlantic shore and the clans of the mountains and the

glens. The Pictish lowlands of Fife and the east coast are palpably different from the Northumbrian Lothians and Borders. And Galloway is another place entirely. To assert that we are all Scots and stick a full stop at the end of the sentence is to miss a great deal.

What I hope this whistlestop tour has also shown is that nothing was inevitable. The Scotland we see now was not always there, waiting patiently to emerge. The periods when Northumbrian English, Gaelic, Pictish, Old Welsh or Norse cultures were in the ascendant should not be seen as diversions. They were possible directions. And no one at the time knew where the road would lead.

Younger, shorter, certainly slimmer, our ancestors looked like us, but they thought about the world differently. The image of the decapitation of the little children in the Sculptor's Cave at Covesea is shocking, certainly, but it's important to recognize that those parents who carried their bodies along the beach at low tide saw it in another way. They were not unfeeling savages, they comprehended the world differently, in ways we don't understand. Shock shouldn't be our only reaction. We owe our ancestors a debt of understanding as best we can, and we mustn't judge them by modern norms.

The brutal execution of William Wallace is easier for us to comprehend. Equivalent atrocities happen now, in other parts of the world. What gives us pause was the judicial, ritual nature of his torture and death. It was sanctioned by the state, by the king of England, and until very recently criminals in this country continued to be put to death by the state.

Wallace's grisly fate is emblematic of a theme that insists on its place. Scotland has been thinking about England for a long time, far more than England thinks about Scotland. Given the relative population sizes, that makes sense, and it continues to be the case as recent events have shown. But when our gaze lifts over the Cheviots and takes in the rest of Europe as well, and the world beyond, our nation flourishes. This is a matter of historical self-confidence. Adam Smith, James Small and J. M. Barrie saw themselves as Scots who were citizens of the world, and not only the neighbours of a much more powerful nation.

The past is rarely a reliable prologue for the present, but it is all we have. A better understanding of our history will help us make better sense of what is happening around us in the early part of the 21st century. And the more we know of the past, the better we will understand who we are, and what we might become.

Bibliography

Geoffrey Barrow, *Robert the Bruce and the Community of the Realm of Scotland*, Edinburgh 2005

Bede, *The Ecclesiastical History of the English People*, Oxford 1991

Anthony Birley, *Tacitus: Agricola and Germany*, Oxford 1999

Tim Clarkson, *The Makers of Scotland: Picts, Romans, Gaels and Vikings*, Edinburgh 2013

Edward Cowan, *Montrose: For Covenant and King*, Edinburgh 1995

T.M. Devine, *The Scottish Nation: A Modern History*, London 2012

T.M. Devine, *To the Ends of the Earth: Scotland's Global Diaspora, 1750–2010*, London 2012

S.S. Frere, *Britannia: A History of Roman Britain*, London 1991

Michael Fry, *A Higher World: Scotland 1707–1815*, Edinburgh 2014

Arthur Herman, *The Scottish Enlightenment: The Scots' Invention of the Modern World*, London 2003

James Hunter, *Culloden and the Last Clansman*, Edinburgh 2010

James Hunter, *A Dance Called America: The Scottish Highlands, the United States and Canada*, Edinburgh 2010

Lawrence Keppie, *The Legacy of Rome: Scotland's Roman Remains*, Edinburgh 2004

Michael Lynch, *Scotland: A New History*, London 1991

Rosalind Marshall, *John Knox*, Edinburgh 2000

Alistair Moffat, *Before Scotland: The Story of Scotland Before History*, London 2005

Alistair Moffat, *Bannockburn: The Battle for a Nation*, Edinburgh 2014

Alistair Moffat, *Scotland: A History from Earliest Times*, Edinburgh 2015

John Prebble, *Glencoe: The Story of the Massacre*, London 2005

Kenneth Roy, *The Invisible Spirit: A Life of Post-War Scotland 1945–75*, Edinburgh 2014

T.C. Smout, *A History of the Scottish People, 1560–1830*, London 1998

Alfred Smyth, *Warlords and Holy Men: Scotland AD 80–1000*, London 1989

W.J. Watson, *The Celtic Place-names of Scotland*, Edinburgh 2011

Index

For Barbara and Marjie Moffat with all my love.

First published in the United Kingdom in 2023 by
Thames & Hudson Ltd, 181A High Holborn, London WC1V 7QX

First published in the United States of America in 2023 by
Thames & Hudson Inc., 500 Fifth Avenue, New York, New York 10110

British Library Cataloguing-in-Publication Data
A catalogue record for this book is available from the British Library

Library of Congress Control Number 2022939652

ISBN 978-0-500-25264-2

Printed in China by Shanghai Offset Printing Products Limited

MIX
Paper from
responsible sources
FSC® C109093

Be the first to know about our new releases,
exclusive content and author events by visiting
thamesandhudson.com
thamesandhudsonusa.com
thamesandhudson.com.au